Words A Potpourri of Fascinating Origins

JA 94

Words

A Potpourri of Fascinating Origins

GRANT CAMPBELL

Illustrations by

DUANE GORDON

CAPRA PRESS
SANTA BARBARA

ACKNOWLEDGEMENTS

Appreciation and thanks are due numerous sources, as indicated in the Select Bibliography, and specifically the following for their permissions to reprint specific material:

CHILDREN OF THE RITZ from "Words and Music" © Estate of Noel Coward 1932, included in *The Lyrics of Noel Coward*, Methuen, London 1983, Overlook Press, New York 1978. Reprinted by permission of Michael Imison Playwrights Ltd., London.

The William Safire quote from the prelude to *Words of Wisdom*, compiled and edited by William Safire and Leonard Safir, a Fireside Book, published by Simon & Schuster, © by Cobbett Corporation.

An excerpt from the Cole Porter lyric "Let's Do It," © 1928 Warner Bros., Inc. (renewed). All rights reserved.

An excerpt from "Ballad of Mack the Knife" by Bertolt Brecht, which appeared in *The Threepenny Opera, The Modern Repertoire,* edited by Eric Bentley, © reprinted by permission of the Indiana University Press.

Data on the shark, courtesy the Monterey Bay Aquarium, Monterey, California.

Bernard Shaw quotes, permission from The Society of Authors on behalf of the Bernard Shaw Estate.

The Burton Rascoe, Peter Finley Dunne and Ambrose Bierce quotes, reprinted by permission of Evan Esar and from *The Dictionary of Humorous Quotations* © by Evan Esar, published by Horizon Press.

Cover design and typography by Denise Eltinge.
Editorial assistance by Cynthia Cornett.
Printed by McNaughton & Gunn.

LIBRARY OF CONGRESS CATALOGING-IN-PUBLICATION DATA
Campbell, Grant, 1927
Words: a potpourri of fascinating origins / Grant Campbell / illus. by Duane Gordon.
p. cm.
ISBN 0-88496-355-1
1. English language Etymology. I. Gordon, Duane. II. Title.
PE15174.C35 1992
422dc20   92-15086

Published by CAPRA PRESS
Post Office Box 2068, Santa Barbara, CA 93120

Table of Contents

A Saying Before

WE KNOW THE meanings of many words. Even if we can't formally define them, we instinctively use many of them correctly or at least understandably. The real fun though comes when realizing how and why a word was born and its later wanderings. That's true meaning. It's also **etymology**. The etymology of etymology is based upon the Greek **etymologia**, from **logia**, meaning reason, study, plus **etymo(s)** or true. Therefore etymology points us to the true sense of a word.

Upon learning I was writing a book, friends or acquaintances offered the usual query as to its subject. Upon hearing etymology, they usually expressed surprise that I was into bugs. I shared in their amazement.

We often confuse the similar sounding etymology with **entomology**. Equating **ent** with **ant** is an easy way to remember that entomology is the study of insects. However, the Greeks, who were bugged about their words, have a more interesting explanation. Their word for insects is **entomon**, from **entomos**, a cut or notch, in turn from **temnein**, to cut. All this because they observed that insects possess notched or segmented bodies. There, we have the etymology of entomology.

Dissect a word as you would an onion. Peel away its outer layer and you catch a tantalizing scent of history, culture, tradition, folklore, perhaps mythology, and a heavy dose of religion and sex. Along the way we trip over the ironical, amusing and enlightening, all while being informed yet entertained.

Words **meander**... from one culture to another, often shading their meaning along the way. We thank the Romans for their **maeander**, and ultimately the Greeks and their **maiandros** for giving us a label to describe this wanderlust. The latter were inspired by the **Menderes** River, noting its winding ways across Asia

Minor before it disappears into the Aegean Sea. Among some of the "meanderings" in the ensuing pages of *Words*:

> The illustrious past of something as plain as an old shoe is hidden in the French word for footwear, their **sabot**, in turn from the Turk's **shabata**. Add -**age** to it and presto, we have **sabotage**. This explains why a **saboteur** was a boot maker of shabby workmanship, as any French peasant in the 16th century would attest when wearing uncomfortable wooden shoes.
>
> It's a given that the **devil** represents a bad guy. But why the appellation devil? Quite possibly, because the **deoful**, Old English for devil, ironically was a god. We had loads of them in those days. This all came about because **deo** is a variant of the latin **deus** or god, that fell, since **ful** is a variant of **fall**.
>
> And down on the farm we find that a struggling plowman and a rhythmical poet are strange bedfellows. The poet cleverly **turns** a line of metrical **verse**, because the idea of verse came to him from the plowman who with his ox turns (from the Latin **vertere, to turn**) to begin another furrow.
>
> Why are we considered broke when out of money? It's literally for the same reason we have **bankruptcies**. A proto-banker, that is, a money changer in medieval Italy, saw his **bench,** or **banca,** used for retaining stacks of coins, broken, or **ruptured**, upon suffering financial misfortune.

We know that an **oxymoron** cuts two seemingly incongruous ways. But why? The Greek **oxys**, meaning sharp, mated with **moron**, or dull, aptly labels a self-contradicting figure of speech. . .as does the partially schooled **sophomore**, who is half **sophos** (clever) and half moron.

Looking behind words takes us back to where it all began, which brings up what began here . . . **A Saying Before**, in true meaning a preface: from the Latin **fari**, to speak, plus **pre**, before.

To shun complexity, footnotes are held to a minimum, and mainly as a cross-reference to chapters that deal with identical words. Similarly, diacritical marks are omitted, since they pertain to phonetic values and offer little value to etymologies and definitions.

No chapters are prerequisite to others, with the possible exception of First Words, which you may wish to peruse first, as it offers a brief overview that traces the development of our language and the origin of the names given many of our predecessor languages. ❧

—GRANT CAMPBELL

First Words

WITH ENGLISH OUR mother tongue, a wonderful world of words awaits our pleasure. On first blush one would expect that most of our words originated in England. Not so. Barely two percent of our words bear a made-in-England stamp. Our language is Germanic.

However, substantiating that English is riddled with complexities, English has borrowed more words from many other languages than it has from its ancestral tongue across the Channel. Nevertheless our Germanic inheritance shows in many of our basic words that we use frequently. One only has to consider the Old High German **guot, bezziro, bezzist**, the modern German equivalent **gut, besser, best** and our **good, better, best** for common examples of English words akin to their German ancestors. And, of course, some like **kindergarten** unmistakably have German written all over them.

Others have been camouflaged by centuries of linguistic metamorphosis. Indo-Europeans[†], whose tongue is the ancestor to languages used by approximately half of today's world population, recognized glimmers of light, their **mer**. It became the Germanic **murky**, later the latter's **Morgen** since the first sign of light appears in the dim of morning. Once the Germans, actually the **Angles** tribe, crossed the North Sea into what we now call England, Old English changed morgen to **morwen**, as did Middle English to **morwening**, as did Modern English, thank God, to **morning**. With this in mind, **Guten** (good) **Morgen**, doesn't sound so strange to the English speaking traveler in Germany.

If so little English is homemade or borrowed directly from Germany, where did most of our words originate? Everywhere. England as an invader, and as the invaded, was a linguistic melting pot that at times boiled over.

Attesting to this explosion of English, Pemaquid Indians of New England greeted pilgrims with passable English of "Much

welcome, Englishman." The Pemaquids
learned their basic English from British
fishermen who visited New England
shores prior to the pilgrim's landing. In
the reverse direction, English by the
mid-1500s had adopted words from
more than 50 languages. Some came
from the American Indian. We took his
arahkunem, for example, meaning
"he scratches with the hands," an
obvious trait of the animal, and

squashed it into a much more manageable **raccoon.** Less
ambiguous is our **hooch,** or liquor, which acknowledges the
distilling expertise of the **Hoochinoo** tribe.

The result of all this give and take: a richness of language and
expression that we share with more than one-third of the world's
population. The French, actually French-speaking Normans,
brought us more than a third of our words (most based upon
Latin, some in turn upon Greek) after their conquest of Britain in
1066. In the process many became Anglicized, e.g., **catalogue** to
catalog, theatre to **theater.** English finally in the 1960s invoked a
portmanteau* word to describe these English-adopted French
words: **Franglais.**

Looking back, though, the freedom-loving French looked to
Germany to conceptualize their national identity, proving once
again language knows no borders. The **Franks** of Germany occupied Gaul in the 400 to 500 era and owe their name to the Old
High German **Franko,** the ethnic name of the ancient Germanic
people of the Rhine.

Those who ruled, the **Frankreich,** enjoyed freedom. But their
French subjects got the idea. The Old French **franc** means free,
liberal, generous, as does our **frank** today mean candid, and definitely free to members of Congress sending all that mail our way.

Just how Franko popped onto the scene is not clear. It may have
stemmed from the Late Latin **francus,** meaning free. Or it may

have derived from the Old Saxon franko, to them a spear, an essential tool for maintaining one's freedom.

Certainly we can't ignore the Vikings, a catchall name for the Scandinavians, including the Danes, also known as **Norsemen** (hence **Normandy** France in recognition of that Viking conquest). Today when strolling along a **firth**, a narrow indentation of the sea coast, from the Old Norse **fjord**; a **fell**, a highland pasture, in Old Norse a **fjall**; or a **beck**, that is a stream from **bekkr**, in England's picturesque Cumbrian Lake District, you are touched with Viking verbal vestiges from eighth and ninth century invasions and intermarriages. You could also walk through a **mire**, (Old Norse **myrr**) a swampy marsh, and that's why we risk becoming stuck, or mired.

Going back just a minor blip in time, several hundred years earlier, we bump into the **Saxons**. It was wise giving these warriors a wide swath. They hail from Saxony, in the Elbe Valley of Germany. In Anglo-Saxon terms they were known as the **seax**, meaning **ax**, hence the Old English **Seaxan**, men of the long knife, who presumably were experts at using same.

Somehow the Angles tribe took most of the credit for **England**, the latter considered a contraction of **Angleland**. Why **Angles**? It's been suggested the tribe's name reflected the area in which it lived, a hook, or angle-shaped area where Germany joins Denmark.

Relatedly **angul** is Old High German for fishhook, as is the relative **ancus** for crooked in Latin and **ankos**, a bend in Greek. Relatedly the Greeks gave us a much larger hook, the **anchor**. Another relative is today's **angler**, our fisherman, who also when "apres-fishing" angles for credit about the big one that got away. If you guess that your **ankle**, which forms an angle between your foot and leg, has anything to do with all this, you are absolutely right.

And, of course, **Latin** was the language of England, at least in government and religious circles, during the Roman occupation of approximately 400 years. Latin is a form of **Latium,** a country-side of ancient Italy. It was probably compounded from the root **lat,** meaning wide, broad, a description once given to Campagna Romana, the open countryside around Rome. Despite the Roman occupation of **Londinium,** little Latin invaded English from that time. Most came later, dressed in French.

It was a German scholar, Jacob Grimm, one of the brothers of fairy-tale fame, who verified for us the connections between related Latin, proto-Germanic and English words. Stripped of complexities, Grimm's law is known as the consonant shift:

p, t and k in Indo-European became
ph, th and kh in proto-Germanic, and
f, th and h in English

Thus, our **fish,** we reason, was expressed as **peisk** by Indo-Europeans. Pre-shift traces show in the Cornish and Breton **pisk** and the Latin **piscis,** the latter explaining our **piscator** (fisherman) and **porpoise,** a pig fish, from the Vulgar Latin **porcopiscis,** or hog fish, from the Latin **porcus,** hog.

In Britain, the Romans couldn't help but notice a tribe that preceded them at least a 1,000 years that was heavily tattooed. Consequently the Romans called upon their verb **pict,** to paint, and named them **Picts,** who merged with the Scots after the departure of the Romans.

The origin of the Picts is a mystery. Perhaps the secret was known by their predecessors, the **Celtic** tribes, from **Celticus,** thanks again to the Romans, who were great at naming all they encountered. The Celts, also known as the **Gaels,** offer an argument to the Angles' credit for England, claiming that it was **an-gael**-land. Celtic fathered Scottish-Gaelic, Irish-Gaelic, as well as Manx, Welsh, and Cornish and its dialects are still spoken throughout niches of Europe.

However it wasn't until 1786 a Celt successor knew the source of his language, Indo-European, spoken by late cave and hut dwellers and the oldest common denominator language yet discovered. Then Sir William Jones, a British judge stationed in India, was studying Sanskrit when he noted that many of its words shared ". . . a stronger affinity with Greek and Latin than could have been produced by accident . . . and they had to spring from a common source."

There is no written record of that source. Reconstructed by linguists, it was called Indo-European and spoken by a people somewhere between Europe and India. Interestingly, no Indo-European root for sea exists, except their **mori,** thought to be a small body of water. This helps substantiate the inland habitat. It was succeeding cultures that became awash in a sea of mori. . .the Latin **mare,** or sea, predecessor of our **marine, maritime** and interestingly the delicious Italian **marinara** sauce. This spicy stuff apparently was most popular among Italian sailors.

The Indo-European **navigated** his inland waterways in his **nau,** later the Latin **navis,** both meaning boat. Early on both the Greeks and Romans equated sea sickness with the pitch and roll caused by rough seas, hence their **nausia,** our **nausea,** for sea sickness, and later by extension to a situation that strikes us as extremely disgusting or repugnant.

Back to our land-roving Indo-Europeans. Their words for beech, willow and wolf and lack of expressions for the Mediterranean olive, cypress and palm suggest a Northern home base. Furthermore they knew of snow (**sneigwh**).

Amazingly, even though what we have chosen to call Indo-European was in vogue around 8,000 years ago, today's Lithuanian can recognize some of the ancient language that they have so well preserved in Lithuanian. All these hints, so some scholars speculate, narrow conjecture as to the Indo-European ultimate base to inland Eastern Europe, probably between the steppes of Russia and Lithuania.

The Indo-European undoubtedly knew farming, as suggested by his words for domesticated animals and plants. Around 3,000 BC words began to flow like rivers, as the Indo-European and his **ekwo** struck out in many directions. The Romans later adapted the ekwo as their **equus**, hence our **equestrian**. Many of his words basked along the Mediterranean and later resided in the continent, undergoing massive surgery or at least face-lifts along the way. As a result the original great mother tongue is much in evidence in not only the Italic and Hellenic, but the Indo-Iranian, Celtic and Germanic families of languages, among others.

Recognizable siblings of the Indo-European **bhrater**, or **brother**, for example, abound . . . Sanskrit **bhratr**; Greek **phrater**; Latin **frater**, which leaves little doubt how we formed **fraternities**; Old Irish **brathir**; Old Norse **brothir**; Old Saxon **brothar**; Old Prussian **brati**; Dutch **broeder**; Russian **brat** and Modern German **Bruder** to name a few.

How did the Indo-Europeans acquire their lexicon? Who knows? There's much speculation. Leading researchers suspect that the Indo-European family of languages was a branch of a previous family, dubbed Nostratic (our language) that perhaps existed 14,000 years ago. Lack of words for domesticated animals suggests that people of the Nostratic tongue were hunter-gatherers. Nostratic, in turn, may be an offspring of the ultimate mother tongue of the world's 5,000 plus languages, referred to as Proto-World.

Interestingly, the branching of languages parallels genetic branching. When homo sapiens commenced their world travels from their suspected home in Africa various groups continuously diverged, never to see or talk with each other again. Thus, reason researchers, their genes changed as did their languages.

And in the event you wonder from whence Proto-World, the bow-wow and sing-song theories are as good as any. They hold that first words were simply echoic of nature. You can loudly yell **boom** and make a case that it sounds like the natural noise that accompanies lightning, **hiss** like the wind, or **buzz**, thanks to the bee. ❧

† Abbreviated I-E in subsequent chapters
* See "In Port"

From The Heart

O NE CAN EASILY imagine an Indo-European venturing forth from his cave or hut to hunt for game with an exhilarating sense of **kerdhe**, that is putting one's (**dhe**) heart (**ker**) into the task. Approximately 4,000 years later Indo-Europeans infiltrated into the Italian peninsula as did kerdhe, surviving in Latin as the similar sounding **credere** with an altered sense of to believe or trust.

Thus the heart pumps more than blood. Figuratively it and its derivatives, developed in many cultures, spared monarchs from being starved or poisoned out of their realms, allows us to borrow money, gives poets a wellspring of allusive grist when expressing the magic of love, all while providing the keystone for religious belief.

Spawned from credere is the Latin **credentia**, or **credence**, referring to something we accept as true, factual. That's because credence in medieval times referred to a pretasting ceremony of foods placed on a sideboard on behalf of royalty. If a tasting servant showed no ill effects from the tasting, diners had credence that the food was fit for a king. We now know the sideboard as a **credenza** (credentia with an Italian twist). All because, "Credence was vsed, and tastynge for drede of poysenynge," as observed one in the late 1100s.

Credere also conceived the Latin **credo**, I believe. It's the ancestor to our noun **creed**, a summarized definition of Christian doctrine. Specifically, this means the Apostles' Nicene and

Athanasian creeds, "The three credes the whyche our moder holy chirche singeth." Another derivative of credere, **recreant**, via the Old French **recreire**, refers to a traitor, in one sense one who goes back (**re**) on his faith. If you don't believe any of this, you're a **miscreant**, an archaic expression for the nonbeliever, often labelled a depraved villain (from credere plus **mes, mis**, a Latin prefix for away or awry).

Associated with ker is the Greek **kardiakos**, the basis of our medical term for the heart (**cardiac, cardiologist**) and the Roman's **cord**, also meaning heart.

We knock bankers as heartless. That's at odds with history. When advancing **credit** (a derivative of credere) the banker literally believes in his heart that you will repay the obligation.

For every creditor there's a **debtor**, from the French **dette**, in turn the Latin **debitum**, the "b" in **debt** a throwback to the Latin form. Excesses of debt are not a recent phenomena. **Felix qui nihil debet**, or happy is he who owes nothing, underscores the sage Roman observation. **Incredulously**, a tally of a debt until the early 1800s in many advanced countries (Great Britain for one) was actually a stick split lengthwise. Both halves were notched to indicate the debt, one given the debtor, the other the creditor.

Upon maturity the halves were matched, signifying **accord**, hearts (**cord**) together (**ac**). If one party altered the stick, obviously that was grounds for **discord**, hearts apart (**de**) . . . but not the derivation of a debtor's admonition to a creditor that he knows where he can stick his debt.

When closing a letter **cordially**, it's with heartfelt or deep feelings. The Latin cord also explains why a **cordial**, as in liqueur, originally was regarded as a stimulant for the heart.

School boys, who carve initialed hearts in tree trunks, and poets know love comes from the heart, because it's deeply felt. Who could express it better than Robert Browning in his "Meeting At Night."

Then a mile of warm sea-scented beach;
Three fields to cross till a farm appears;
A tap at the pane, the quick sharp scratch
And blue spurt of a lighted match,
And a voice less loud, through joys and fears,
Than the two hearts beating each to each! ✺

Flows The Don

MANY SNAILS AND crustaceans carry their houses wherever they wander. Lexically, when we venture forth, we also lug a household load of handy and familiar concepts for describing the world we encounter.

Just a few of the thoughts the I-E house, **dem**, including its variants **dam** and **dom**, conjure up such disparities as the Lord, the Madonna, all kinds of madams, gangsters, a masquerade ball, a parlor game, tutors and school masters, the Canadian government, dungeons, and even sexual deviates.

The house, a Latin **domus**, logically is run by a **dominus**. In its most simple form it grew into an Italian **duomo** and a Middle French and English **dome**, atop some houses and later many churches, public buildings and eventually railroad cars . . . per the portmanteau **vistadome**.

In your **domicile**, possibly crunched from the Latin **domo** plus **cola**, a dweller, you are the master . . . as is the Lord and God the **Dominus** of the house of worship. His Lordship reverberates throughout the litany:

• **Benedictus Dominus**, "Blessed be the Lord," lit
erally is to speak well of him. . .**bene** (well) plus
dictum, something said, from **dicere**, to speak.

• **Dominus vobiscum**, "The Lord be with you",
vobis (you) plus **cum** (with).

Our house provides a hood-like shelter over us. So is a **domino**
a hood worn by priests in a **monastery**. The latter's rich history
deserves an aside. It's from the Late Latin **monasterium**, formerly
the Greek **monazein**, meaning to be alone (**mono**) as often is
the **monk**. That's not much fun for most of us. . .as Jean Paul
Sartre noted, "If you are alone and feeling lonely, you are in
bad company".

Back to our priest's hood or domino; the French borrowed the
word and extended it to describe a costume worn at a ball and later
a small mask. That series of events left us with a guessing game to
determine how domino was extended again to the game. Most
favored explanation is that the master, that is the **dominant**
player, wins the game. Also advanced is the illusion of the dots
imbedded on domino tiles to the domino wearer's eyes showing
through his mask. Or, if you prefer, one who wore a domino was
jokingly mocked as one who looked like the priest who **dons** a
hood. (The latter don is not related to our household don family,
but is derived from **do** plus **on**, as is **doff** from **do** plus **off**.)

Domino theory (or effect) proponents had it all wrong. Knock
down the first domino standing in a row and they will all fall in
lock step, as most kids discover before discovering how to play the
game. But today instead of one country after another going communist we have communist sovereignties falling all over themselves
trying to forge democracies.

The Roman dominus sired the Spanish **don** (and Portuguese
dom) respectful titles representing Mr. or Sir, and by inference a
lord, if not a gentleman. The don is also a head fellow or tutor at a

university, as well as a head of a family, or in the Mafia, a crime syndicate.

The Romans twisted the **domin** stem of dominus to **dominari**, to master, that is, to **dominate**. Likewise, the Middle Latin compound **praedominium** gave them a way to describe a supreme power, one who **predominates**, a self-assumed habit of many males.

Not surprisingly **Don**, as a given name, courtesy the Celts, means powerful. If **trump**, as suspected, is a variant of **triumph**, then Donald Trump is a redundancy.

Donnas shouldn't be too harsh over their opposites' long-standing bias to predominate. Some experts contend that it was bred into them long before they realized their predominance. Pushing Darwin's ideas on natural selection back further, new theories claim that sperm from multiple partners can live for up to 10 days within a woman, while competing for the prize of an egg. Kamikaze sperm have been observed to band together to barricade some sperm to provide interference for other superior sperm in their quest of the egg. Undergoing such rigorous competitive trials so early in the game offers males a rationalization for their predominant stance.

But donnas need not despair. In their subtle, seductive ways females influence the outcome. The unfertilized egg sends out chemical signals that can actually turn a favored sperm's head and start his vigorous swim up the fallopian tube, leaving competitors ruthlessly behind. This biochemical handkerchief dropping suggests that male predominance isn't all that dominant!

As a sperm craves an egg, a Roman dominus needs a **domina**, a mistress of their domicile. Entering the domain of domina can lead to all kinds of strange bed dominas. Domina begat the Italian and Portuguese donna, **dona**, in turn **madonna**, or my lady, a title of respect, the revered **Madonna**, the Virgin Mary, and the pop-porn Madonna who indignantly accused the Vatican of regarding her in whorish terms.

Domina gave speakers of the Old French the idea of the **dame**, a title of respect, like our Mrs. Relatedly they came up with **madame** (**ma** from the Latin **mea**, or my). Madame was clipped to **madam**, still a respectful term in 1300 for a woman of authority, and definitely by the 1700s a requirement for any madam that ran a brothel, a house but not a home.

Joining the latter pejorative connotation, we have the **dominatrix**, who has loads of tricks hidden up her sleeve. By definition she is a dominant woman. And her role has been extended as the dominant player in a sadomasochistic sexual relationship.

Sadomasochism, sexual gratification by inflicting or receiving pain, appears sad to many but has no connection with that adjective. It's a redundant eponym. Marquis de Sade, a French soldier and novelist, practiced it and Leopold von Sacher-Masoch, an Austrian novelist, gets the dubious credit for identifying the condition. From the double eponym we not only derived the term **masochist**, but also **sadistic**.

It's also **dangerous** playing with dons and doms. For example, **D.O.M.** is a long-standing expression for "To God, the Best, the Greatest" from the Latin "Deo Optimo Maximo." Yet many dictionaries carry the slang **d.o.m.**, properly consigned to the lower case for dirty old man.

D.O.M. has been most successfully transformed into a secular success, a liquor that has prospered for almost 500 years. **Benedictine** liqueur originally was made by French monks led by St. Benedict in the 16th century, and is still made and bottled in France, which speaks well (the Latin **dicere**, to speak, plus **bene**, well) of the Benedictine Company and their Benedictine and Brandy.

Back to danger. It hails from the Anglo-French, Middle French **dangier, dongier**, in turn from the Vulgar Latin **dominarium**, equivalent to the Latin **dominion**, a lengthy process to prove that danger's original meaning hinged on the concept of jurisdiction. In other words, our dominus held jurisdiction over his domus. Breaching that jurisdiction at your peril explains why the meaning of jurisdiction gave way to the connotation of danger.

That ill-advised act might land you in the dominus' **dungeon,** from the Middle French **donjon,** and guess what, from our old dominion. That's because the dungeon was the most secure part of a medieval castle, a place of protection for residents in the event the castle was breached, but its basement usually reserved for outsiders caught dangerously violating jurisdiction.

Implicit in dominion is the power to rule, as do the British Empire's self-governing dominions, such as Canada, which elicits many an argument in Quebec. We share the power to govern common facilities in **condominiums,** often the root of arguments in many condo home owners' associations. . .all this leaving scant argument that there is a household world of words out there. ❧

Spreading Some Salt Around

S ALT, NOW REVEALED as a culprit in causing hypertension, a condition affecting around 35 million Americans, is definately "out." But think how long it was "in." The first salt mines, according to archaeologists were discovered around 6500 BC in Austria, and today those caverns, near **Salzburg,** the "City of Salt," are a major tourist attraction.

Our word for the ubiquitous spice came from the Latin **sal,** or **salere,** to salt, which sired many offspring, including the Vulgar Latin **salsa,** the Old French **sause** and our **sauce,** usually made with salt and originally contained in another sal descendent, the **saucer.** So craved our taste for the zesty salt it inspired our names for a number of dishes, that are salted, including **sausage†, salami** and **salads.**

And prior to refrigeration we pickled meat and fish with salt to preserve it while adding flavor. Possibly less preserved and definitely less reserved in modern terms is one in the sauce or pickled sense, both slang terms for the intoxicated.

Romans gave their soldiers allowances (salt money) to buy salt. These stipends, referred to in Latin as **salarium**, gives us our term **salary**. We also can thank the Romans for the expression **worth your salt**. Their value of salt is exemplified by Roman **Via Salaria,** the "Salt Way," the road from Rome to the Adriatic Sea salt mines.

Salt became a symbol of worthiness and power, per this notation from the *Literary Gazette* of 1842: "To dine like kings, queens, potentiates and other salt of the earth." Epitomizing salt's status was the allusion that table service without salt in 16th–century England was worth a cuckold's fee, if the offended diner wanted to claim it . . . **cuckold,** a derisive label pinned on the husband of an unfaithful wife was probably inspired by the cuckoo's habit of laying her eggs in another's nest.

The customary **saltcellar** in the middle of a 17th-century dining table marked a line of status: "Hee (who) humbly sate Below the Salt, and munch'd his Sprat," obviously was a commoner. Not so obvious is the redundancy of the compound saltcellar. The suffix is not a storage area for salt, but instead was derived from the English **saler,** an earlier word for saltcellar, and like salt a descendent of the Latin sal.

Attesting that with salt we add zest to more than our food, it once was a prime ingredient in the preparation of holy water added to coffins to discourage intrusion by the spirit of the salt-hating devil and also sprinkled into mash during its brewing to keep witches at bay. And still today, kids are subjected to the frolicsome bird-catching myth, "It is a foolish bird that staieth the laying of salt on hir tail."

With its metamorphical meanders it's not surprising that salt has flavored politics. Instead of being rowed up the Ohio River to

Louisville for an important address in the presidential campaign of 1832, a boatman rowed candidate Henry Clay up the river's tributary, the **Salt River**. He lost Kentucky and the election. Like Clay, many a candidate has been rowed up Salt River at the hand of alleged dirty tricksters.

In slang form salt symbolized value. To salt an invoice was to exaggerate its charges, a forerunner of the modern practice of "cooking the books." Gold mines in Australia were salted by sprinkling gold dust around an unproductive hole to favorably sway an unwary buyer.

Spilling salt once invited the threat of the ominous: "If the salt thou chance to spill, Token sure of coming ill." As a conciliatory gesture to ward off these evil spirits you threw salt over your left shoulder. (If Madison Avenue could resell that custom, homemakers would be sweeping the stuff off the dining room floor, and salt marketeers could care less about any market loss from hypertension concerns.)

Lowly salt has even conquered nations. Rome, tiring of Carthage's many attempts at conquering it, including Hannibal's elephant-mounted troops, finally put an end to this mischief by destroying the enemy's ability to grow crops. Romans simply laid Carthage's land barren by poisoning it with salt. That would be wise strategy (with a grain of salt) for the Pentagon. Imagine, laying low our enemies with bombers of salt without killing a soul . . . all the while opening up new export markets for our bumper crops! ❧

---

† See "Culinary Concoctions: Eponyms III"

Who "Dunnit?"

EDGAR ALLAN POE, THAT'S WHO. With his *The Murders in the Rue Morgue* in 1841, and other perplexing challenges solved by Monsieur C. Aguste Dupin (in turn a model for Arthur Conan Doyle's Sherlock Holmes) the **mystery** story genre was launched.

The mystery of mystery, however, takes us much further back than Poe's era. The Greek's have their **mysterion**, a secret religious ceremony, derived from **myein**, to shut one's eyes, as the yet uninitiated were not permitted to view such ceremonies, which to them remained something not understood, baffling. Both took their mysterious turns from the I-E root **mu**, that is the sounds of mutter, jumble . . . the meaning of which was most difficult to **detect**.

Detectives galore, Poe's successors gave us, who literally uncover for us the mystery of who "dunnit." They derive their title from the Latin **detectus**, the past participle of **detegere . . . de**, or un, plus **tegere**, to cover. Their mission to uncover, of course, does not preclude adopting a **cover**, or secret identity, or perhaps engaging in **covert** action, all this subterfuge a lineal descendent of the Latin **cooperire: co**, to, plus **operire**, shut, cover.

We also call them **police**, which has lots to do with a **metropolis**, its **politicians** and their **policies**[†]. Call them **cops**, though, and we are presented with a mystery fraught with all kinds of false clues. Police uniforms of England's bobbies once were adorned with **copper** buttons. Cop has been advanced as an acronym for **constable on patrol**. A cop ultimately reports to a **chief of police**. All these possibilities, however, belong to the realm of folk etymology.

Rather, the experts suspect that cop is a slang derivative of the Latin **capere**, to seize, catch. . . a prime duty of one who wears the badge. Holmes, like Dupin, usually beat the cops at their own game of catching: "My dear fellow, it was all perfectly obvious from the beginning."

A special breed of dog served as the inspiration of a commonly invoked appellation for detective, the **sleuth**. Sleuth is a contraction of **sleuthhound**, the Scottish bloodhound respected for its dogged pursuit of suspects. The name of the breed came to us by way of the Old Norse **sloth**, a track or trail left by the pursued.

We look to England, however, for the detective's tactic of **eavesdropping**. In Middle English, the compound noun, spelled **eavesdrop** and also **eavesdrip**, described water not only dripping over **eaves** of a house, but also the ground below where it ran off. Therefore, it's understandable how eavesdrop evolved into a legal permit required prior to construction of a residence if water was expected to drip from eaves onto a neighbor's land.

From the 15th century on, however, mystery afficionados stole the term to describe our detective who hides behind the eaves, clandestinely **investigating** his case. He gets there by searching for footprints, a step back to the Romans and their **vestigo**: to follow a footprint, as when searching for clues.

This brings to mind that when searching for **clues** we are literally gathering threads of evidence. To speakers of Middle English a clue was a ball of thread, as was the Anglo-Saxon **cliwen**, **cleowen**. And those who spoke Common Germanic were all balled up in **kleuwin**. You can follow this thread back further to the Sanskrit **glaus** and ultimately to the I-E **gleu**, **glou** and **glo**, all equating to a ball or lump. But to unravel all this we turn to Greek mythology, namely one named Theseus, who volunteered to proceed into a cave in Crete, ostensibly to be sacrificed there along with other youths in an annual rite at the hands of **Minotaur**, a fearsome hybrid of half man and half bull. (It's no bull to equate the suffix -**taur** with the Latin **Taurus**, the astronomical bull.)

Back to the myth's main thread, which is exactly what Ariadne, the King's daughter and Princess of Crete, having fallen in love with Theseus, gave him. She also wisely gave him a sword. After slaying Minotaur, Theseus followed the thread he trailed behind him when entering the caves to serve as a clue on the way out of the labyrinth.

As with many myths we are mystified over its ending. One version claims Theseus upon his return spurned Ariadne's affections. Another holds that the couple sailed away: O'er the ocean blue. Where to? Nary a clue.

When obtaining evidence cops are searching for the obvious, that which is clear. That's because the Latin **evidentia** evolved form **videre**, to see. (Remember veni, **vidi**, vici? . . . I came, I saw, I conquered . . . one of the most bandied about sentences in high school Latin and reputedly Caesar's succinct summary of his 47 BC victory over Pharnaces, the king of Pontus.)

What could be more handy when gathering evidence than a **stool pigeon**. Blame a mangled culinary presentation of buck-shot pigeon for this highly descriptive term. So one story goes, an enterprising British pigeon hunter solved this problem by lashing a tame pigeon's leg to a bush and waiting nearby with a net to capture harmlessly another pigeon upon being attracted by the live decoy.

Standing around awaiting the prey taxed our hunter's patience. Thus evolved the use of a stool. The pigeon's leg was lashed to it, and the hunter was afforded a place to comfortably relax. And accordingly we inherited the term stool pigeon to describe one who informs on his peers.

Catching crooks in England once was not the exclusive prerogative of cops. All citizens joined the hunt, a tradition inherited from the Normans. A noisy pursuit it was, which left us a vestigial (there's that footprint or trace again) **hue and cry**. Hue, from the French **huer**, to cry out, made it redundantly clear that one answered the call, in full hue and cry and joined in the chase of a suspected felon.

To not do so was to risk arrest until hue and cry laws were rescinded well into the 19th century.

Catch the pursued and you can expect cleverly contrived **alibis** to substantiate he was elsewhere other than the scene of the crime. Alibi, the noun, evolved from alibi the Latin adverb, meaning elsewhere, as did the noun **alias**, a false name or circumstance, derived from the Latin adverb alias, meaning otherwise.

You could call his alibi a **falsehood**, a story in itself. Time was when thieves were more deceptive about masking their identity than simply wearing masks. Distinctively fashioned hoods of garments identified ones calling, that of doctor, priest or artist. A con artist simply disguised himself in the cloak of respectability by wearing a **false hood.**

Clever these thieves, also known as **crooks,** as their character basically is bent, as decreed by crook's Old Norse progenitor **kraka,** or hook. One type of crook, the **burglar,** reveals as much about his actions as he does his whereabouts.

Those whereabouts evolved from an I-E **bhergh,** a hill, thence a fort. Attesting to the universal need of fortresses are the Old Icelandic and Saxon **burg,** Old English **burh,** Middle English **burgh** and Modern German **Burg,** or castle. Forts became cities, as exemplified by **Pittsburgh** and **Edinburgh.** Forts also became **boroughs,** as are the divisions of New York City. Relatedly the rabbit and fox when seeking refuge **burrow** their **burrows.**

And along another path came the Latin **latro,** or thief. When lumped with burg, it yielded **burgulator,** later our **burglar,** who unlike the legendary highwayman, plies his trade nefariously in town.

Coming to the burglar's aid or defense (**defence**) is the **fence,** slang for one who receives stolen goods, or **contraband.** Contraband says it like it is. **Ban** hails from the Middle English **bannem,** the Late Latin **bannum,** and is akin to the Greek **phanai,** Sanskrit **bhanti,** all sharing the I-E **bha,** to speak. The Spanish and Italians married it with **contra**, against, to form **contrabando**. (Relatedly we speak out against the **bandito** in Italy and South America and strive to **banish** the **bandit** in English speaking countries.)

Much of modern law enforcement is focused on contraband drugs. Yet the scourge of drugs has existed so long in some societies that it is difficult to separate the legends of fiction from fact. In 11th-century Persia, fanatics reputedly drugged from chewing **hashish,** a hemp plant, took pleasure in slaughtering Christian Crusaders while in route to the Holy Land. They were known by the Arabic **hashshashin,** abusers, that is hashish takers, in Middle French as **hassassis,** and in Medieval Latin as **assassinus,** which evolved to the English word **assassins.**

Some etymologists question how a narcotic that calms could excite the Muslim fanatics into murderous rampages. One theory rationalizes that the Old Man of the Mountains that led this fanatical band rewarded his addicted troops with hashish only after their slaughter of the Christians.

The modern scope of **narcotic** encompasses sedatives and stimulants that are habit forming. However, its origin is strictly benumbing, from the Greek **narkotikos,** or numbness, and entails mythology and psychology. In the early 20th century English psychologists adopted **narcissism** as a term describing extreme self-love and -fascination . . . as did the Germans several years earlier with their **Narzissismus.**

All this came about because an exceptionally beautiful flower child named **Narcissus,** per a Greek myth, found he could love no one, despite the advances of many, except his own image, which held him entranced beside a reflecting pool. It was none other than **Nemesis,** the god of retribution, that tricked Narcissus into falling in love with his own image. Apparently Nemesis, in Latin a "dealing out," was dealing justice to Narcissus for spurning so many suitors. Eventually the gods tired of Narcissus and metamorphosed him into a flower of his own name.

Myth, character, and author, all diverse but the same, each known with fame but tainted with shame . . . Narcissus drugged with his image, Holmes a victim of a cocaine habit, and Poe, an alcoholic, his life tragically snuffed out at 40, never more the raven at his window nor a rapping at his chamber door. ◆

† See "Whence Politico-Americana"

Righteous Predominance

"**G**ENERALLY THE MOST **dexter** in spiritual matters are sinister, in temporall businesse." That's not a commentary on contemporary Jim Bakkers, who charge like hell for a bit of heaven, but a 17th-century observation having lots to do about **right** and **left.**

Thank the Romans for much of this. Their **dexter,** or right, equated to strength, dexterity or manipulative skills and its meaning extended to favorable omens of the right. **Sinister,** Latin for left, refers to the weakest hand for the majority and its sense extends to ill-omened, inferior, clumsy, and inept. The Romans were not the only ones to regard left-handers as out in left field. This prejudice finds its way into the German **linkisch** (unhappy) the Spanish **zurdas** (wrong way) and the Italian **mancino** (dishonest) . . . all twists on the basic sense of left.

So strong was this superstition favoring right versus left that guards stationed at the entrance of Roman buildings reminded visitors to enter with their right foot foremost, else bad luck would ensue.

Our right stems from the Anglo-Saxon **reht**, in turn from the Latin **rectus** meaning straight (as in the sides of a right angle) and also to rule (or perhaps a king's divine right to govern wrongly). The ruling sense was spawned from the I-E **reg**, meaning to move in a straight line, that is directly, an attribute of one who leads or rules. Why **rectum** for the terminal section of an intestine? Because it consists of relatively straight muscle fiber.

Our left is derived from the Anglo-Saxon **lyft**, originally meaning weak or worthless. Since the majority is right-handed, this predominance was assumed to be right or correct, and the left hand was assumed the weaker with its sense expanded in a continuum of negative connotations . . . awkward, sinister and evil.

The French in lock-step gave us **adroit**, from their **a droit**, meaning with the right hand. Interestingly their **le droit** means the law, something one better be on the right side of. In contrast their **gauche**, or left, gives us our gawk or gawky.

Included once among the rights of those possessing the right to rule in France was a feudal lord's right of sex with the brides of his vassals on none other than their wedding night. **Droit du seigneur**, right of the lord, also known in Roman times as **jus primae noctis**, right of first night, were eventually settled by a monetary payment to the lord in lieu of his "rightful" exercise. It all proves that these bosses lived **en grand seigneur**, in lordly style, and that sexual harassment was practised long before Professor Anita Hill and Supreme Court Associate Justice Clarence Thomas squared off on Capitol Hill.

One possible explanation for the positive connotation of right over left lies in our feudal past. We guarded our heart with a shield held in the left hand and wielded our sword with the right hand. This same school speculates that the Latin dexter, **dexteritas**, skillfulness, adroitness at using the hands, stems from the Aryan **de**, to point, adroitly as with a weapon. **Ambi-** (both) **dexterous** implies that one is double right-handed. Similarly **laevus,** another Latin word for left, is from the Aryan root **le,** meaning bent, as is the left arm when holding a shield.

Perhaps all this bears on the clumsiness, wrongness and worthlessness extended senses of left expressed in so many languages. Some historians claim left-handed warriors were killed at a disproportionately higher rate than their right-handed cohorts, because they did not hold their shields over their hearts.

A 16th-century male-to-female allegation, "Your sex was never in the right, y're always false or silly," by today's standards is a **left-handed** remark. And 200 years later Susan B. Anthony's proclamation on the other side of the Atlantic, asking "How can consent of governed be given" if the right to vote be denied, underscores that women's rights were left out in the cold for sometime . . . and that right was whatever the strong proclaimed.

Best not be a bride of a left-handed marriage. Getting your arms around your wedding present would be like embracing a mirage. Once such a marriage was termed morganatic, that is the bride too far beneath the groom in status, and thereby titles and property could not be given her the morning after the ceremony, as was the custom when status was equal. By default the bride received the morning as a gift... from the Latin **matrimonium ad morganaticum,** marriage toward morning. Fittingly, the groom extended his left hand during the ceremony.

More recently we have the right politically to lean right or left. It possibly started with the French national assembly of 1789. Their **right-wing** conservative nobles sat to the right of their presiding officer (as in place-of-honor to the host's right) and the **left-wing** liberals to the left. This seating arrangement of status quo members on the right and liberals on the left applies to most legislatures in Europe and is replicated with our Republicans on the right and Democrats on the left in both houses of our congress.

Some are right for the wrong reason. Take the **right whale**. Many whalers did and named this slow swimmer such, because relative to other species, it is easy to kill, more buoyant and therefore hauled in with less effort.

If right is so favored, why do the British drive on the left? They may have overcome superstition for a very practical reason that far predates the automobile. A right-handed knight (as were the majority) would have a frightful and awkward time wielding a lance over the top of his mount when charging his adversary. Therefore he's right to ride on the left. ⊷

Of Boots & Sabots

G ETTING THE BOOT can elicit pain or its antithesis, pleasure. Such is the peculiarity of this homonym, a term for words of identical pronounciation and often the same spelling, but of different meanings.

The "pain" boot, same word as the "footwear" boot, is derived from the Middle English and Old French **bote,** in turn from the Latin **bota.** The "pleasure" boot unrelatedly stems from the archaic Anglo-Saxon **bot,** as in the English better, probably a descendent of the Aryan **bhud,** or good.

Being fired, or kicked out, from one's job can be painful. However, getting the boot in 18th-century Scotland was excruciatingly painful. "Shall I draw on him a Scotch pair of boots, Master, and make him tell all?"

This entailed a metal device wrapped around your lower legs with screws or shims being tightened until you confessed, lest your legs be shattered. Of more recent vintage is the Denver boot.

Equally immobilizing, it's applied to your illegally parked car in some localities, cleverly requiring you to pay your fine before being able to drive your car.

On the other hand (or foot) what could be more pleasurable than suddenly gaining a quick profit, or as a pirate would say, capturing the booty. "What will you **boote** bytwene my horse and yours?" probably refers to the monetary adjustment a 14th-century Englishman sought when trading down.

The footwear boot version fits many occasions. On the rear step of a horse-drawn English carriage stood the footman, possibly so named because polishing the boots of his passengers was one of his tasks. Also a compartment located at the rear of the coach was termed a boot, which explains why the English equivalent of our automobile trunk is a **boot**. It seems that coaches were surrounded by boots, as chronicled in the early 1700s: "The Rouges sallied out and charged the Coach at either boot."

Nautically **boots**, or boot camp, are derisive terms, created by rugged salts of yore who customarily mustered on deck barefoot regardless of weather, unlike soft recruits that needed the comfort of footwear.

Dealing in weaponry without the required license, or plagiarizing a copyrighted work, is an act of **bootlegging,** a term popularized by prohibition era moonshiners who carried corn liquor in flat bottles that could be carried hidden from the law in one's boot.

The arduous struggle of putting on high top boots often required pulling on the boots' straps. Therefore succeeding by one's own efforts is pulling one's self **up by the boot-straps,** as if defying gravity or pulling oneself off ground zero. **Booting** a computer, that is hitting a few appropriate keystrokes to initiate an automatic loading sequence of operating system code, is a more modern application of bootstrapping.

Why do we **bet our boots?** Probably because in our frontier days, our good boots, when worn in unfamiliar, and perhaps unfriendly territory, were regarded as survival gear. As with life, bet them only on a sure thing.

When did we start all this booting around? Historians claim around 1100 BC when the Assyrians realized that equipping their barefoot military with boots made them better warriors. (Roman and Egyptian armies escalated gradually, first to sandals, then to boots.)

Boot has a tenuous link to bottle. The Latin **bota** means hide, the raw material for both boots and early bottles, as in bota bags, the Spanish goat skin wine bag.

Another piece of footwear, the French **sabot,** or shoe, derived from the Turkish **shabata,** and combined with **age,** interestingly gave us the term **sabotage.** It's reasonable to presume that wearing wooden sabots marred, or sabotaged, that is -**aged** many a floor. Likewise, tossing a sabot into machinery could easily sabotage a factory. But the connection between shoe and willful destruction goes back much further.

The uncomfortable wooden shoes of French peasants were often of poor quality, hence a **saboteur** was a bootmaker or cobbler with a reputation of poor workmanship. The term became associated with shoddy workmanship in any craft. However, extending sabotage to mean deliberate destruction surfaced later, around the turn of this century, during intense French trade union-management unrest. Ironically, railroad shoes, devices that hold rails to wooden ties, were cut by labor during a strike against French railroads at that time. ⊷

Passing The Buck

I T DEFIES IMAGINATION that we can use **buck** to describe varied actions, such as escaping responsibility, sawing logs, gambling against great odds, and playing football . . . to identify various males, like spirited young men, running backs, Indians, and the lowest of army rank . . . to refer to sundry things such as money, saws and protruding teeth . . . and even to characterize emotions, like cheering up.

From the Old English **bucca** (he-goat) or **bucc** (male deer) and the Middle English **bukke**, the buck and his horns color-fully pervade our lexicon. As the deer leaps, arching its back in the process, so does a football running back **buck the line.** The sense of **buckish** therefore extends to a spirited, dashing young man. Male or female, if your spirits are high or you're cheerful, you are **bucked up.**

Buckskin of a deer served as a substitute for money among American frontiersmen and Indians, hence the slang **buck** for a dollar bill and relatedly the fast buck artist . . . as well as the old double entendre questioning whether the squaw would come across the river for a buck.

It's speculated that the ten-dollar bill's slang attribution of **sawbuck** stems from the x-crossed legs (symbolizing a Roman numeral ten) of a saw-buck, used for holding logs while sawing or bucking them.

Buck privates and buck sergeants are the lowest of their respective ranks presumably, because they enjoy no status other than their maleness (a bit of tired logic that a woman would **buck** in today's army).

A poker-playing, riverboat-gambler of America's frontier days knew it was his turn to deal the cards when a buck-horned knife was placed in front of him. To avoid the deal he passed the knife to the next player, and thus we have **buck-passing**, a euphemism for avoiding responsibility. Extended to office work, we now have the **buck-slip** we attach to paper work, directing it to a bureaucratic peer, thus escaping responsibility while cleverly putting the heat on the recipient. The higher one's rank, presumably the less the opportunity for buck-passing, as exemplified in President Harry S. Truman's legendary desk-top sign, "**The Buck Stops Here.**"

Ironically one can employ the concept of **bucking** when assuming responsibility, as when bucking a head wind while piloting an aircraft, strongly objecting to an issue by bucking it, or perhaps working harder and blowing your own horn when bucking for a raise. Hopefully the latter effort later would prove successful, a leap forward, truly reason to **buck-up**. In contrast, to buck the odds, or in Chaucer's words "to blowe the **bukkes** horn," is to labor in pain . . . which shows how far the buck has come since the 14th century. ❧

Footprints

T HANK THE CRANE that you have lineage, or a **pedigree**, itself a descendent of the Old French **pied-de-grue**, literally foot of a crane.

This allusion came about because marks of succession used on genealogical charts resemble a three-pronged impression of a crane's foot... or a Y, the top extensions representing parents, the **foot** the ensuing issue. "Some fetching their pedigree from the Goddes, and some from the devils", recalls our early recognition that not all pedigrees were **impeccable.**

The pedigree of foot, indicating something underlying as are our feet, is extensive, and reaches back to its Latin roots of **pes** and **ped**; Greek of **pous, pod**; and the I-E ped. We looked down at our feet and came up with all kinds of disparities. In addition to pedigree, we found disgraced statesmen, medical practitioners, pilots, acrobats, soldiers, salesmen, sinners, those with a penchant for using long words, and fishy as it may appear, a mollusk.

Interestingly, our first (early 18th century) sense of the **pedestrian**, formed in English from the Latin **pedester**, portrayed one known for being dull, prosaic, unimaginative, and not capable of soaring to fancy-free heights in his prose, let alone poetry. Only in the latter part of the century did we characterize this chap with his feet on the ground and then not in the complimentary sense of exercising solid judgment, but more in a lowly, goes-it-on-foot connotation as does the pedestrian foot-soldier, or with an Old French twist, the **peon.** He walked into Spanish-American usage as a peasant. He also became a **pawn**, the lowest order in a chess set, and one who is manipulated by others.

This brings to mind a most professional manipulator, a fellow skilled at getting his foot in your door, the salesman, also known as a **peddler**. His pedigree, however, is not on solid footing. Some experts claim the obvious, that he solicits on foot. Others maintain he is an offshoot of the Middle English **pedde**, a wicker basket in which the peddler supposedly carried his goods.

Making his appointed rounds makes him a candidate for a **pedicure**, a French word composed of **pedi** plus **cure**, ultimately from the Latin **curare**, to take care of. Of course, this brings up a professional that we can't help but look down on while he is attending to our feet, the **podiatrist**, from the Greek root pod, plus **iatros**, or physician, who once made a monkey of us. His specialty was earlier known as **chiropody**, as the chiropodist treated both the **cheir** (hand) and foot. This outmoded word was handed down from the obsolete **cheiropoda**, formerly a classification for mammals with hand-like feet that can grasp.

Another handy practitioner is the **chiropractor**. As the suffix indicates, he performs his magic by hand, but considers his methods most **practical**, the latter sense emanating from the Greek **praktikos**. Strangely these professionals, unlike most health specialists, omitted from their calling their area of expertise . . . that is manipulation of the spine. One could advance the case in Latin that they really engage in "**manuspinalis**" (manipulation plus spinal).

Then there is the **pediatrician**. Another member of the ped family? That would be **faux pas**, false step. The pediatrician shares the iatros suffix, but its ped is formed from the Greek **paid**, or child.

And for some fancy footwork we have the **trapezist**, who is a little tricky to decipher. This aerial artist is from the Latin **trapezium** and Greek **trapezion**, because he performs with a four-sided gadget, **tetra** (four) plus **peza**, a modification of the Greek root pous or foot.

Attesting to footprints fossilized all over our linguistic landscape is another obscurity, one who operates a ship. The Greek **pedon**, a steering oar, a relative of pous, was picked up by the Italians as

piloto and later the French as **pilote**, our **pilot**. Best guess is that the Greek's equated the steering oar, located at the foot of the boat, to feet that direct the boat to a desired destination.

So far we have traveled far with our feet. But we also get all tangled up in our feet. One of the earliest restraints placed upon us was a shackle or chain about our ankles, known in Old English as a **feter**, not surprising because of the Old English **fot** (plural **fet**). It's also a cognate of the Old Norse **fjoturr**, akin to foot and the Greek **pede** and Latin **pedica**, both predecessors of the English **fetter**.

This explains in current English why one is **impeded**, from the Latin **impedere**, that is to shackle one's foot and thereby inhibit movement. Literally our foot is freed from a trap when we act **expeditiously**, from the Latin verb **expedire**. And if we want to tie up some big game, why not go after a head of state? The late Latin **impedicare** gave us the idea of tangling someone's feet (ped) in a trap (pedica) or fetter. The French picked up on the idea as **empeechier**, later their **empecher** and our **impeachment**, the presentation of charges of a crime against an official.

Not so serious a fault is a **peccadillo**. Here the Spanish got into the act with their **pecadillo**, influenced by the Latin **peccare**, to stumble, or walk badly, and a diminutive of the Spanish **pecado**, thus a small sin. Hence in Christian terms we are "not walking in the ways of the Lord" when guilty of a peccadillo.

Better we **mind our P's and Q's**, an expression rife with folk explanations. One emanates from the reign of France's King Louis XIV, an era known for extreme emphasis on social graces, manners, dress and elaborate hair styles. Therefore, when attending a royal ball guests were admonished to mind their **pieds** and **queues**, the latter a Middle French word we borrowed for wigs.

Queue is from the Old French **cue**, in turn the Latin **coe**, both meaning tail . . . later adopted in the world of fashion to describe braided hair, more recently a line of people awaiting service, and in the computer age, a sequence of events scheduled for processing, proving that technocrats will invade any domain to glamorize their world of bits, bytes and bauds.

(Interestingly, **coward** also sprung from the Latin coe, probably because the coward calls to mind a scared animal that turns his tail between his hind legs when running in fright.)

Back to P's and Q's. We mind lots of them when engaging in **sesquipedality**, that is using words literally a foot and a half long . . . from **pedalis,** of the feet, prefixed by the Latin **sesqui,** equivalent to **semi** (half) plus **que** (and).

Give an American Indian full credit for a rambling sesquipedalism. The name he gave to a Massachusetts lake is Chargoggpagoggmanchauggagoggchaubunagungamaugg. Translated: "You fish on your side, I fish on my side, nobody fish in the middle." Getting a handle on a word like this is like fettering an eight-footed **octopus.**

JUNK Et All

"A MERICAN WOMEN HAVE loaded them selves with so much 'junk' jewelry they jangle as they walk," so observed a 1960 edition of the United Kingdom's Sunday Express. We are awash in **junk,** including bulk mail pitches that often are trashed unopened. One wonders how much the cost of first-class postage could be lowered if it were not burdened by subsidizing unsolicited bulk junk mail.

We can add to this debased list junk bonds issued by a publicly held corporation to raise funds for a take-over defense, or conversely a raid; food that's considered low in nutrition and often high in calories; unsolicited calls from boiler room operations touting investments or donations; and of course, an old standard, junk pitches, those slower, unusual pitches that can deceive a batter, such as a knuckleball or forkball; and a recent entry, space junk, spent missile debris floating around in space.

Though of obscure origin, junk was introduced into our lexicon aboard ship. Old or worn rope and cable was referred to as junk by sailors. Cut into short lengths junk could be recycled into reef-points for holding shortened sails in place during rough weather; into fenders for protecting a ship when rocking at a dock; into gaskets for keeping hatchways water-tight; and into oakum, untwisted junk pressed into service for caulking plank joints.

Small wonder sailors derisively applied junk to meat, preserved in salt for long voyages. Sometimes its appearance mimicked junk, as presumably did its taste.

Not related, but definitely more tasty is **junket,** a sweet custard made with flavored milk, so named because it was originally prepared in a rush basket, known as a **jounquete** in Old French, in turn from the Latin **juncus** (a reed) plus **ette.** An essential element for an outing the junket became equated with a picnic or a feast. Still later we extended junket to describe a trip, especially when mocking politicians who enjoy the fruits of contrived excursions, often leaving the taxpayer with a bitter taste.

Although a junket could be taken on a Chinese **junk,** again there is no connection. The vessel, noted for its square sails, high stern and flat bottom, is related to similar ships . . . the Portuguese **junco** and the Malaysian **jong.**

And finally, **junk** was introduced in the 1920s as slang for heroin, as was **junkie** for a dealer or the addicted. Still no connection with the junk above, unless we can presume the junkie was trying to tell us something about the deleterious stuff he was pushing.

We almost always associate junk with what's old, worn out,

like a **junker** of a car, a mile short of the scrap heap. A **Junker** to the Germans though is an entirely different matter. He was a member of the aristocracy, often a candidate for the military and young, as the Old High German **juncherro,** that yielded the Modern German Junker is equivalent to **junc,** or young, plus **Herro, Herr** or sir.

But let's not disparage old junk. "Well, I guess I can't call him an old fool any more," observed the wife of a Minnesota fisherman, who stored his old fishing gear in jars in a back yard shed. One of his handmade 3 ¹/₂" lures (patented in 1859) recently sold for more than twenty thousand dollars!

Familiar Relations

W HAT IS THE ORIGIN of the **family,** typically comprised of our most **familiar** of relationships? "It starts with a young man and a girl falling in love; no alternative has been found," quipped Winston Churchill. More definitively, "It's a unit composed not only of children, but of men, women, an occasional animal and the common cold," offered Ogden Nash.

Historically, both miss the mark. Family, from the Latin **familia,** originally identified the slaves and servants of a household, as its predecessor **famulus** meant servant. A wife, possibly acquired in conquest, and ensuing children were simply undifferentiated, as they also served the master. Not until the early 19th century were these kin of the master able to cast off servants to their own kind.

Now more civilized in our amorous pursuits, family formations start with a **suitor,** from the Latin **sequor, secuts,** meaning to

follow, as does a boy pursue his girl. Their honeymoon **suite** also stems from the suitor word family, as a suite equates to one room following after another. And if later irreconcilable differences arise, and the marriage is viewed not as a word, but a sentence, one spouse may file a **suit** as plaintiff against the other.

The wedding ceremony was once known as a **bride-ale,** from the Anglo-Saxon **brydealu,** a combination of **bryd,** the **bride,** or woman about to be married, and **ealu,** that is ale. The pledge or vows of marriage were sealed with a cup of ale. The bride-ale connotation of a wedding feast eventually was pummeled to **bridal,** and later was accepted as a noun or an adjective.

To simplify all this, our couple could run away. That's exactly their act, per the Middle English **alopen,** its prefix **a** signifying the beginning of an act, in this case **lope,** to run, from the Dutch **lopen.**

How does the **bridegroom** fit into all of this? Folk etymology interestingly latches onto the Persian **groom,** a male servant who cares for horses, and extends him as a servant to his bride during lengthy rural European wedding feasts. It's not quite that simple, according to etymologists. Bridegroom hails from the Scots **brydgrome,** an alteration of the Old English **brydguma,** bryd plus **guma,** for man. Guma eventually was transformed to **gome,** then **grome,** and finally groom.

Why colloquially are the bride and groom tying a knot? It's a throwback to an almost extinct custom in many societies that the dignitary performing the marriage ceremony when blessing the spouses would actually tie together two corners of their wedding garments to symbolize their new status.

The **honeymoon** we take bears only a scant relationship to our **honey** (mate). You have deep affection for her, or him, per the Old English **hunig,** akin to the Greek **knekos** and I-E **knkono.** Essentially these meant something sweet, as is the honey the bees give us from the nectar they collect from flowers. All this may conjure memories of feeble hints of sex education directed at children in terms of the birds and the bees. As Cole Porter put it, "Birds do it, bees do it, even educated fleas do it."

Our term for the first celebrated days of marriage, known originally (in the 1500s) as the **hony moone**, stems from a German custom of newlyweds partaking in mead, wine made with honey, for approximately a month after the ceremony. So much for the cynical derivation of love waning a month later, like the moon.

To **wed** is to pledge, but as many a party to a marriage gone sour will attest, it's also a gamble. Prior to its marital sense, to wed was to **wager**, Middle English for a pledge in the form of a bet. The sense later expanded in the marital sense "to **weddian** for fairer, for fouler." **Wedlock**, contrary to what folk etymology may profess, is not a pledge frozen in perpetuity with a metaphorical **padlock**. Rather this -**lock** is the rare, perhaps only current, use of a suffix that simply means activity, in this case "plighting one's troth," that is truth. Hopefully **plight** here is the verb (from the Middle Dutch **plihten**, to guarantee) and not the noun, as it would be awfully early in the game to find one's self in a sorry **plight**.

In his preface to *Getting Married*, Bernard Shaw stated the odds rather unattractively: "When two people are under the influence of the most violent, most insane, most delusive, and most transient of passions, they are required to swear that they will remain in that excited, abnormal, and exhausting condition continuously until death do them part."

Bride and groom once **betrothed, be,** plus **treuth** (again, for truth or fidelity) pledge their loyalty and become **spouses.** The latter stems from the Old English **spuse,** in turn from the Latin **spondere,** to bind solemnly. This explains the promises underlying our **sponsorship** and the **responsibility** therein entailed. Ultimately spouse derives from the I-E **spend.** Spend a spouse can do, often to the chagrin of another, but in the I-E sense it meant to promise. The Greeks picked up the word as **spendo,** their pouring of a libation, to seal many a business promise, or contract, with a glass of wine.

Our couple is also known as **husband** and wife, the former likened to fires by Zsa Zsa Gabor: "They go out if unattended." Actually, he's a product of the Anglo-Saxon **hus**, or house, plus **bonda**, a freeholder. That's because commoners once lived in serfdom, in cottages owned by their masters. To own land was an inherited privilege or one granted as a reward for extraordinary exploits.

For girls, a husband was a highly coveted prize. By the 13th century, any married man, be he owner or renter, became known as a husband. As the manager of the household, thriftiness and prudence were among his virtues; thus developed the sense of **husbanding** resources. "A good gorunde ... well husbanded bringeth out great plentie of byg eared corn," captures the spirit.

The **wife**, or **woman** of the husband, derives from Old English **wifman**, from **wif** plus **man**. The latter originally equated to the sex-neutral human, in this case a female human being. Wifman gave way to all sorts of variations, including **wimman, wummon, wumman, womman** and finally woman. Wif also connected as **husewif**, eventually altered to **hussy**, now a bawd who maintains a brothel, and whose duties are a far pejorative cry from those of a housewife.

Homemaking duties of a housewife have much to do though with a lady, despite the refined, polite and well-spoken attributes credited her by our modern dictionaries. Ladies owe their heritage to their barely recognizable Old English ancestor **hlaefdige**. Like so many Old English words, if you stare at hlaefdige long enough its modern equivalent, lady in this case, presents itself. It's a combination of **hlaf** (loaf) plus **-dige**, a variant of **daege** (kneader) and relative of the Old Norse **deigja** (maid) all explaining the original preoccupation of the fair sex.

Ladies need not let men **lord** this bit of unsavory history over them. The arrogant master also has a lexical skeleton in his closet. Lord derives from the Old English **hlaford**, who was a mere loaf keeper.

Loaf keeper aside, some etymologists think man's greatest attribute is that he thinks, assuming man descended from the I-E **monus**, meaning the thinking creature. Perhaps if he had thought more about it, he would have restricted the sense of **man** to the neuter **human**, or collectively **mankind** and **humanity** and not ascribe man to males. We would have been relieved of modern feminism's awkward **spokespersons**, **mail-persons** and the threat of **person-hole covers**. The Old English didn't suffer this problem. Along with wif for female, they tidied things up with **wer** for male.

(Wer is related to the Latin **vir**, which explains all kinds of manly characterictics . . . including **virtue**, a moral excellence, as well as the **virtuoso**, one with a specialized skill notably in a form of the arts. Now these terms are no longer sexist. Not so, however, with **virility**, with its senses of physical strength and capability of procreation.)

As to our wer, he's almost an extinct species, now found only in **werewolf**, a legendary man-wolf, which brings us back to the wolfish, rapacious characterization many a wif held for her wer and the family of slaves they begot.

Kinky

MANY STRAIGHTS AND gays don't buy each others sexual attitudes. But they can agree that sex among some lower animal forms is indeed bizarre. Perhaps **kinky**, a twist or turn in one's nature, is the more apt adjective.

Consider these twists in animal sex. Male angler fish, in their dark ocean floor habitat, seek a partner from a sense of smell and luminescence of the typically much larger female. Copulation starts with a literal bite into the side of the female, the last bite the male will take. No divorce possible from his sometimes polygamous partner; he's hooked for life, possibly along with another male in a relationship befitting the descriptive French term **ménage à trois** . . . house of three, commonly used to describe a situation wherein three share not only a common abode but sexual relations. He fertilizes her eggs. Her circulatory system gradually replaces his, and he eventually becomes literally absorbed by his lover.

The French picked up menage from the Latin adjective **mansionaticus**, of a household, in turn from the Latin **mansio**, or mansion. Menage is related to **menagerie**, a place for wild or unusual animals, sometimes on exhibition, which brings us back to what some characterize those of a ménage à trois.

Take the nautilus, a crustacean of the deep, for unconventional sex. His entire reproductive organ is severed during mating, deposited inside his mate's mantle pouch. It regrows, however, in preparation for his next encounter.

Ranking high on bizarre sexuality is the oyster.[†] Many varieties undergo sexual reversal during their life span . . . some doing so seasonally. A female European oyster tucks its ova into a muscle fold in its cavity, then converts to a functioning male, thus carrying embryos. . .as a pregnant male! The oyster's confusing sexual orientation was put succinctly in a limerick by Berton Braley:

> *According to the experts, the oyster*
> *In its shell or crustacean cloister*
> *May frequently be*
> *Either he or she*
> *Or both, if it should be its choice ter.*

Legendary are some species of salmon that perpetuate their kind at great effort and extreme sacrifice. At breeding time their genitalia are activated by a transfer of chemical substances from outer muscles. As a result, their skin becomes spongy. They change color, from silver to grey and brown. The male takes on large black spots, also irregularly shaped red and white spots. Its front teeth become larger, its jaws elongated, the lower turned upward, its appearance perhaps mimicking its determination to defy the challenge of finding its spawning ground.

Having traveled several thousand miles through the ocean to miraculously find (some say because of a keen biomagnetic compass) the coastal stream of its spawning, then swimming perhaps another thousand miles inland to its ancestral headwaters, at times leaping vertically several lengths more than its own length to conquer rapids, dodge hungry bear and elude luring fisherman, going through the exhaustive spawning metamorphose, all this while fasting along the way, then in many cases succumbing in exhaustion, says something about the fanatical propagation instincts of the salmon! Even in afterlife the salmon contributes to the continuation of its species, as nutrients of its decaying carcass drift downstream eventually to settle in a lake as grist for the survival of its progeny.

Credit, if not sympathy, the blue crab deserves for a seemingly exhausting mating ritual. Upon finding a female ready to molt her shell, a male will cradle her underneath him by hooking his claws and legs beneath her. He carries his lover in the cradle fashion for approximately three days until she sheds her shell.

After this arduous undressing, actual mating takes place, and sometimes lasts up to 12 hours! The male must kick his legs, sometimes furiously, to establish a current to carry his sperm to the female's sacs. Then the male resumes transporting his partner, again in cradle, until her shell hardens. The female lays her eggs from two to nine months later.

Just the thought of this laborious process is enough to turn one into an old crab, the female doing just that, ambling off to die within a year after spawning. Somehow the male manages to hang on for another two or three years of molting and mating.

For sex-to-end-all-sex, we can look to the swifts, swallow-like birds noted for their rapid flight and maneuverability. Uniquely they copulate while airborne, spiraling and nervously fluttering their wings while descending. The swifter the better as the ground approaches . . . too late for the headache routine, but time enough to offer an excuse if there ever was one, for faking a climax. ᴥ

†See "Metaphors Of The Sea"

The Synergism of Symbiotism

RECENTLY VOGUISH IS the resurrection of **symbiosis** to describe modern business relationships, as for example *Fortune* magazine's characterization of General Motors' Saturn and its suppliers as **symbiotic.** In so doing the editor is borrowing from our perception of nature and attempting to glamorize the inanimate with the animate.

The word is derived from the French **sym,** or **syn,** (meaning together) and the Greek bios (life). Examples of more prevalent and classical usage, pertaining to two natural organisms (also known as **symbionts**) living together and often attached, are downright fascinating and ingenious. Symbiosis may be termed **mutualism,** that is mutually beneficial, or **parasitism,** in that case advantageous only to one of the players, at the expense of the other.

The use of **parasite** to describe the invader is a story in itself. The Greeks used their **parasitos** to describe one who eats at another's table, usually as a reward for flattery directed to the host: literally, **para,** around or beside, plus **sit(os),** grain or food. We later transposed the feeding-beside sense to describe one who takes advantage of another without returning any favors.

Mutual "backscratchism" abounds in the marine world. Sea anemones, for example, fire toxic cells at predators who even lightly brush the anemone's tentacles. The paralyzed prey then is consumed by the anemone. However certain fish, such as the clown, are immune to the anemone's sting, and therefore live near the anemone, free from predators. An attractive and colorful fish, the clown serves as a "stalking horse" to attract unwary prey within lethal reach of the anemone. The latter repays its dues. The clown conveniently lives off the egestion of his host.

Certain shrimp perform a cleaning service for larger fish, removing fungi, damaged tissues and thus help relieve sores. The shrimp, in turn, ingest the removed debris. Larger fish have been observed to queue at cleaning time, often physically jostling for position at cleaning stations established by the shrimp. At the same time they protect the shrimp from any natural predators lurking nearby.

The bloodthirsty crocodile[†], who consumes practically any creature within its range, has a very practical understanding with the plover bird. It grants the plover dispensation from its customary lethality by allowing the plover to remove leeches and other debris from the crocodile's teeth in return for a free meal. Obviously the plover has a tremendous incentive to perform its oral hygienic duties diligently.

And for a who's-on-first scenario we can look carefully to a rare pair: the medusa (a jelly fish) and the nudibranch (a sea snail). As observed in the Bay of Naples and chronicled in Lewis Thomas's *The Medusa and the Snail*, the snail carries a small parasitical blemish near its mouth. Nothing noteworthy here except when we realize the parasite was none other than a miniature medusa jelly fish.

Now events turn bizarre. Though permanently attached to the snail the jelly fish reproduces, its offspring eventually growing into a mature jelly fish. Not to be outdone the snail produces larva, that once grown into a very young snail, finds itself ensnared within the tentacles of the menacing jelly fish.

But the trapped snail turns the tables on the jelly fish. It's now payback time for all those generations-in-residence by the jelly fish to the detriment of the snail's facial profile. The snail starts gnawing away, first at the jelly fish's canals, later its tentacles, growing in size from this nourishment, as its prey withers to almost nothing.

Almost, because the jelly fish's legacy is its eventual parasitical spot along the side of the victorious snail's mouth . . . this odd couple set for another generation of symbiotic punch and counter punch.

Definitely parasitic is the relationship of a small snail, called the oyster drill, that exists at the expense of some crustaceans. He wields a rather unique food gathering mechanism, an "outboarded" rasp, or radula, that combined with occasional bursts of its self-secreting lubricant, allows it to bore holes through shells of oysters, muscles and clams.

Another savvy pair of symbionts are mites and moths. The former nests in one ear of the latter, purposely leaving the other free from obstruction lest the moth not be able to detect an approaching bat that preys with all its might on moths with all their mites.

On shore, what could be more practical than the symbiotic relationship of the zebra and the ostrich. The former possesses a keen sense of hearing, the latter excellent vision. Realizing their respective strengths, they often prowl the territory together to warn each other of impending predators, such as lions, to improve their chances of survival.

The result of this mutualism: **synergism,** from the Greek **synergos,** that is syn (together) plus **ergos** (work). . .meaning that the result of combined efforts is greater than that achieved by working separately, a two plus two equals five situation. ⌖

---

†See "Looking Ferocious"

Big Wheels

Y OU COULD SPECULATE that a bureau, or a chest, became a place where bureaucrats could hide their dirty linen. However, it did not happen that way.

The origin of the word **bureau**, from cloth, is as interesting as its evolving connection to **bureaucrats** and their **bureaucracies**. Bureau, obviously French, not so obviously comes from the old French **burel**, a coarse, woolen cloth that was used to cover writing desks, which collectively became known as bureaus. (Bureau as a chest of drawers for holding clothing was a secondary usage.)

The transition from bureaus to bureaucrats and bureaucracies was natural, and with a rather demeaning connotation. For example, President James Garfield in 1880 complained about the lack of action from a bureau because of the "weight of congressional influence pressing for the appointment of men, because they are our friends." Simply put, the inoperative was the operative.

The negative connotation was not exclusive to the United States. In 1843, The *United Irishman* refers to a bureaucracy as an "inveterate evil of Ireland." A *Daily News* article of 1870 talks about "That bureaucrat love of classification, which is the curse of France." A year later the same periodical refers to a ministry "with all its routine of tape, wax, seals and bureauism."

Before the advent of binders, red tape was used to bind and preserve documents in an orderly array. Thus the term red tape evolved as a bureaucratic attribute. According to national archivists we inherited the practice from the British, who forwarded us official documents, like the famed Stamp Act, bound in red tape. Preservation, however, proved elusive. Many documents from the last century, unlike bureaucracies, are fading away because of the acid content of their red tape.

Today our bureaucracy encompasses much more than bureaus, as in the Census Bureau. There are close to 400 federal agencies listed in the code of federal regulations . . . whether they be services, as in US Postal; departments, as State; offices, as Copyright; boards, as Contract Appeals; committees, as Endangered Species; associations, as GNMAE; plus assorted authorities, administrations, commissions, systems, foundations and corporations. What next will our bureaucrats conjure?

Bureaucracies don't die easily. In what was Soviet Russia about four percent of the arable land is farmed privately and produces approximately a fourth of the crops. Logically, expanded privatization of the vast, inefficient collectivized farms would substantially lower the cost of food, and relatedly enhance the standard of living of citizens of the newly confederated states. But the agriculture bureaucracies, faced with loss of centralized power, won't buy it, nor will peer bureaucracies buy the threatening precedent.

Nor is a bureau solely the province of government. A New York publisher of trade journals can have its West Coast bureau (but hopefully not a bureaucracy). Credit bureaus and travel bureaus abound. My California State Auto Association insurance policy asks that I think of them not as a company but as a bureau . . . all because of a piece of brown cloth.

Even older than the Old French burel for coarse cloth is the recorded rare and obsolete use (in 1325) of **burel** as a spoke of a wheel. No valid connection is this burel to bureau, but it does call to mind a fractured beatitude: Blessed be our bureaucrats who run in circles, for they shall be known as wheels! ❧

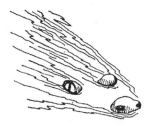

Looking Ferocious

T HAT QUALIFYING AS **ferocious**, per lexicographers, must merely appear as such to the beholder. It's based on the Latin **feroc,** meaning fierce, plus **-oc,** related to the Latin **oculus,** or eye.

An all-pro Giant defensive end, crashing through the Forty-Niner offensive line, understandably could appear ferocious to quarterback Joe Montana. Similarly, the perceived ferociousness of a snarling, agitated pit bull, even under owner's leash, could force a bystander to the other side of the street.

Call him menacing, frightening, ruthless, blood-thirsty, or any of the above, my vote for the most naturally ferocious creature is a **crocodilian** . . . the salty alligator, who cleverly compounds its savagery with cunningness and allegedly hypocritical behavior.

Crocodilian comes to us from the decidedly less menacing worm or the lizard. The Latin **crocodilos** is based upon the Greek **krokodrilos,** in turn from **kroke,** pebble plus **drilos,** worm. That's because the Greeks in the fifth century took note of the lizards, or pebble worms, that basked along rock-lined river banks.

The **alligator** designation for these large lizards derives from the Latin lizard, **lacerta,** which the Spanish exported to the New World as **el lagarto,** eventually smashed by Americans into alligator.

Back to the salty. Even from safe vantage the salty appears ferocious. A yawn exposes numerous intimidating teeth, all the more ferocious when one realizes that he bites with a force of 3,000 pounds per square inch. His horny skin of partially ossified armor plate is grotesque. The salty's ferociousness though is more than skin-deep.

What appears in an Australian mangrove swamp as a protruding rock or bump on a submerged log, for example, may not be that benign. It's possibly a **Crocodylus Porosus**, or salt water alligator, lurking in its quiet, motionless observation profile, with only the top of its knobby head barely above water.

The rest of the reptile, weighing up to a ton and measuring up to 30 feet in length, is cleverly hidden beneath the water's surface, thanks to a unique ability to properly distribute air throughout its lungs. Once an unlucky prey, even one as large as a hippopotamus, or savage as a lion, wanders too close to water's edge for a drink, all 2,000 pounds of the **crocodile** is airborne within seconds, its massive jaws gripping the doomed prey. Suddenly, the ferocious crocodile performs its legendary death-role, flipping its victim under water to drown it, prior to tearing it apart and devouring it.

Known as salties, because their glandular system excretes excess salt, the reptile is comfortable swimming in the ocean. Some have been reported to have swum more than 1,000 miles. Today its main habitats are the shores of India, New Guinea, the Philippines and Australia.

The salty has been ascribed powers beyond its capability, such as cleverly mimicking cries for sympathy to trap the unwary. Hence the fabled expression, **crocodile tears.**

In Australia salties have overturned canoes, as well as small power craft by using their powerful jaws as leverage on the boat's propeller or its shaft. Dumped passengers are indeed lucky to survive a terrifying swim to shore.

Perhaps the ultimate massacre by salties was a WW II incident reported in 1945 from Ramree Island in Burma. There approximately 1,000 Japanese soldiers, badly mauled by British troops, tried to escape annihilation by a nighttime retreat through a mangrove swamp. Hidden from view and acutely alert were herds of salties, previously driven off shore by the din of fire power.

The Japanese eventually became mired in the muddy swamp. The scent of their bloody wounds began to excite the crocodiles. Rather than waiting for daylight to attack, as would the British, one reptile after another sprang out of the darkness, evoking horrifying screams from their prey that startled the British troops stationed well off the swamp. Surrender the night before would have been a wiser course. Only 20 Japanese survived.

An off-shore swim in salty country may look inviting, but best not go near the water. That log may be more fierce than what meets the eye. If, though, you hear cries for sympathy, shed no tears. Cheer up. You're asleep, dreaming.

Panning Around

How thoughtful of the Greeks to give us their god, **Pan**, who has sprouted all over our lexical landscape. Pan, portrayed symbolically in Greek mythology as a hybrid man (upper torso) and goat (lower), was god of all nature–pastures, forests, flocks and herds–and one to reckon with. Unexplained noises of the forest were ascribed to the wrath of Pan, thus causing **panic** among mortals in the sense of groundless alarm.

It was none other than Pan who panicked the Persians into a hasty retreat in the battle of Marathon (in SE Greece), so say the Athenians. And that's why we have Marathons, 26-mile, or 42-kilometer runs, emulating one Phiedippides, who ran from Marathon to Athens to relay the news that the Persians fell to the Greeks in that famed battle in 490 BC.

In the modern sense we can **hit the panic button** for many reasons. Just ask an investor with heavy long positions when the Dow Jones Industrial average collapsed 500 points in one day's trading. Or recall the **pandemonium** (uproarious confusion) that broke out in brokers' back-room operations in trying to handle the avalanche of sell orders. (Milton in his *Paradise Lost* gave us pandemonium, a combination of pan (all) plus **daimon** (devil) the author's term for the capital of hell, where Satan and his peers resided.)

Unfortunately there's no **panacea** (from pan plus **akes** meaning cure) or universal remedy to protect us from the price gyrations of triple witching stock, stock index and future options all expiring simultaneously and magnified by program trading.

Panacea, the daughter of Aesculapius, god of medicine, certainly had the right intentions, starting us down the road of universal cures. However, some of our contrivances appear a little hard to swallow. As late as the 1600s one consisted of ". . . saffron, quick silver, vermilion, antimonie, and certain sea shells made yp in fashion of triangular lozenges." All this of course supports a late 14th-century observation that "Physitions deafen our eares with the Honorificabilitudinitatibus of their heauenly Panachea."

And, for a can of mythological worms there is **Pandora** and her legendary box. Her story starts with Prometheus and his theft of heavenly fire and its transformation to life. This feat upset Jupiter, who in turn commanded Vulcan (the gods' mechanical arranger) to create the world's first woman, whose mission was to plague man. (Men at that time were Titans, born from the bowels of the earth, a convenient way to explain the lack of the opposite sex.)

Vulcan complied by creating Pandora (from all plus **dora**, gift) who received from each god a special power that could destroy man, real overkill for a pyrotechnic infraction by the one Prometheus. The powers (among them, jealousy) were contained in a box given Pandora by the conniving Jupiter. Prometheus, smart enough to handle fire, understandably was leery of the box. But not so his brother, Epimetheus, **pansophism** (or universal wisdom) definitely not one of his distinguishing traits. Upon his marriage to Pandora he opened the box and out flew all the afflictions and tribulations of man. Thus, beware of the dilemma represented by Pandora's box. It's a trap disguised as a gift.

Perhaps with a degree of literary license, this vignette on pan can be termed a **panorama,** or series of unfolding observations. The primary usage of panorama refers to a comprehensive view of a wide area: Pan plus the Greek (h)**orarma** (sight). **Panning the scene** with a camera therefore captures a continuous series of pictures. Done so in color requires using **panchromatic** film (**chromato,** a combining form for color).

Pan homonyms abound. We **pan,** or make a face, perhaps **deadpanning** in an unemotional manner. Not a bad idea if you strike it rich when **panning** for gold (separating it from gravel by agitating it in a pan) and wish to keep your vein secret by feigning calmness. Thanks to California mother lode lore, events successful have **panned out** well. Not so, though, when we jump from the **pan** into the fire. Our critics can **pan** us for that.

A pan is a cup, vessel or container which lexically begets beggars, or **panhandlers,** who hold forth their pan or cup to collect coins or food. Thus the panhandler avoids contact with his benefactors. Why no contact? Perhaps begging once was associated with untouchable lepers.

To **pander,** however, is not to panhandle. The panderer provides a service in return for a reward. Pander is an eponym and flows from Pandaro, a character in a poem *Il Filostrato* by Boccaccio (1340) and later Pandare of Chaucer's *Troilus and Criseyde* as well as Shakespeare's Pandarus in his *Troilus and Cressida*. All three characters arranged for clandestine encounters between lovers. Shakespeare's Pandarus sets the stage for pander, per his admonishment, "If you ever prove false one to another, since I have taken such pains to bring you together, let all pitiful goers-between be

called to the world's end after my name; call them Panders."
Now **panderism** pejoratively is associated with arranging illicit sex, or pimping. ✒

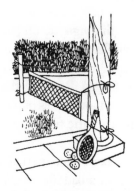

Stretching
a Point

DESPITE THE CURRENT rage of
stretching prior to physical
exercise, we are far more preoccupied
with figurative stretching. All this fun-
nels back to the I-E root **ten**, predecessor to the Latin **tendere** to
stretch, a relative of **tenere**, to hold . . . something conditioning
coaches encourage their charges to do with a stretch.

Tenuous is the connection of stretching with the game of
tennis. Like a **tent**, so called because it is stretched over a frame,
the game could be named for the strings stretched over a tennis
racket, or the net **extending** across the court†.

However, most etymologists **tend** toward the "**Tenetz!**" school.
This Old French term, meaning hold, receive, take, was called out
by the server to alert opponents that service was forthcoming.

More tidy yet is the theory that tennis is an eponym for the
Egyptian delta city of **Tinnis,** known in medieval times for its
quality linen that was fabricated into the finest of tennis balls. Still
another theory suggests tennis derives from the Arabic **tanaz,** to
leap, a feat often required when returning a volley.

Interestingly, the game's progenitor was known by the racquet,
not the ball and originally was named **jeu de paume**, the palm
game, simply because the ball was batted with the palm of the of
hand. The obsolete French **raquette** meant palm of the hand,

derived from the Arab **rahat**, all this explaining why we hit a tennis ball not with a club or bat, but with a **racket.**

When tennis was imported to England from France make-shift courts were contrived by extending a net across a courtyard, often from a pillar near the entrance of a castle to a post supporting a gate. As the player was driven from pillar-to-post across the court, so now we are when **attending** to one problem then another.

Interjecting a **double entendre** (borrowed from the French to express one word **intended** to convey a double meaning, one often risque) love meaning no-score in tennis is certainly at odds with a lover, whom the world knows scores. A zero-score or goose-egg, is expressed in French as **l'ouef,** but corruptively pronounced love across the channel. If you can't swallow the egg theory another explanation holds that a player with a score is in-the-money, in contrast to the zero-scorer, who is in the game only for love.

The French are given credit for inventing the game sometime between the 13th and 15th century, depending upon the version of le jeu. Understandably its lexicon had ample time to develop its share of ghost terms, words spawned accidentally. A serve, nullified by the ball striking the top of the net and falling into the opponent's service court, customarily is termed by the ghost term netball. Technically it's a **let ball,** from the Old English **lettan,** a derivative of **laet,** related to the Old Norse **letja.** These archaic terms mean to slow, delay, hinder, something a let ball does to the game, a far cry from our contemporary let, which signifies to allow, as is the server allowed, to commence another serve upon a let ball.

A **tendency** to play the game too often invites a **tender** elbow, the former an inclination to, the latter resulting in soreness or pain, both representing a doublet, or words that took different routes from a common root, in this case the I-E ten.

A more serious affliction, **tendinitis,** may or may not have anything to do with tennis. But it has lots to do with an inflamed

tendon composed of dense fibrous tissues that stretch between the muscles and the bone. It's from the Greek **tenon**, a relative of the Latin tendere.

Not of tendons is a **tenderloin**, a tender, that is not a tough, cut of meat that runs through the sirloin. A district in New York City became so known after the Civil War because of the corruptive practice of bribing police was so prevalent. The cops lived high on the tenderloin, though they **ostensibly** pledged to uphold law and order.

Ostensibly (stretch plus **os**, a variant of **ob**, meaning towards, thus expose) one wears a seventy thousand dollar, diamond-studded Rolex watch to ascertain the time. More likely this **pretension** masks an **intention** to impress others that the owner can afford such a luxury.

Thus an **ostentatious** display of wealth can **portend** the **unintended**. More than a few wearers of Rolexes have been advised to **tender** their watch with the words, "Your watch or your life," spoken from behind the chilling reality of a gun barrel. As cloth or a tent is stretched to the limit and held taut on a tenter, or framework lined with hooks, so too the victim's anxiety painfully is stretched, putting him on **tenterhooks.**

It seems as though we are continuously in a holding or stretching state. Consider the **tone**, that is, the pitch of your voice. Tone derives from the Greek **tonos** (strain) based upon **teinein** (to stretch) which is exactly what we do when straining for a high note – stretch our vocal chords.

However, at times we "unstretch." Government spokespersons trot out a word for it when characterizing tensions between nations as relaxing . . . **detente.** ❧

[†] See "Barnyard Justice"

Taking Liberties

W HAT A CONVOLUTED PATH a root can take to give us such incongruities as a gentleman of the arts and a debauched rogue . . . all this while branching into bark, paper, and the enlightenment of books and even libraries. Throw in the story of an opera and what became the legal concept of libel.

Top it off, if you wish, with a glass of wine. All, thanks to the Romans and their **liber** (our free) or **libertas** (our liberty) and their **liberalis** (our liberal).

Their liber was a free man. By the middle ages the **arts liberalis** described an education befitting such a gentleman and included grammar, dialectic, rhetoric, music, arithmetic, geometry and astronomy. These seven categories acknowledge biblical authority, as in Proverb Nine: "Wisdom hath divided her house, she hath hewn out her seven pillars." Hands-on, mechanical duties were for the socially inferior (arts servile). Even law and medicine were considered too practical for gentlemanly pursuits, which proves that some professionals, who can really zap your budget, have come a long way.

The Latin **libertus** was a man freed from slavery. The word evolved into the French **libertine**, which by the 17th century conveyed the idea of freedom to extremes, as exemplified by the **Libertines**. They were a free-thinking sect, and rationalized that all is God. He can't sin, therefore we can't and anything goes. Unfavorable reaction to the licentious behavior of the Libertines eventually ended their brief reign of advocacy.

Liberty, Equality & Fraternity, as a motto for the French revolution, has a nice ring. For more than 100,000 Frenchmen, however, in the wrong place at the wrong time, it was **liberticide,** the loss of their liberty, from the Latin **cidium** (the act of killing) in turn from **caedere** (to cut down).

Libety of one may be tantamount to tyranny of another. So cautioned Lincoln: The shepherd drives the wolf from the sheep's throat, for which the sheep thanks the shepherd as his liberator, while the wolf denounces him for the same act . . . plainly the sheep and the wolf are not agreed on a definition of liberty.

Today's liberal is characterized by open-mindedness, tolerance, lack of prejudice and a disposition toward political reform. Therefore a **libber** advocates a cause, as in women's lib.

Appropriately **Liberia,** an African republic, was founded for the reparation of slaves freed from America in the early 1800s. Its capital, Monrovia, honored US President James Monroe.

A homonymic **liber** is the inner bark of a tree, specifically in a papyrus plant its pith or core. (The Greek **papyros,** later the Latin **papyrus,** turned up in France, not surprisingly, as **papier,** thus our **paper.**) Getting to the pith of the matter, this material was dried, pressed, then used as media for writing. A collection of libers became books, a collection of the latter a **libarius,** or our **library** (liber plus **ary,** or pertaining to).

Another material adopted for writing was the bark of the **beech** tree, in Old English **boc,** suspected by some with linkage to our book. The designation of a book as a volume predates all other idiomatic uses of volume, such as sound and bulk. The I-E **wel,** used in describing anything rolled, invaded Latin as the verb **volvere,** to roll, and as our noun **volume,** something rolled up, as once were a book's parchment or sheets.

Best not be a subject of a little book, or **libellus,** a diminutive form of liber. Taking liberty with facts and spreading malicious accusations once was communicated in the format of pamphlets or little books. Thus our **libel** was formed from the appearance, not the content of these books. Not so damaging, but in some plots equally unbelievable, is another diminutive of liber, **libretto**, a text of an opera.

Often confused with liber is **libra**, the ancient Roman pound, hence our abbreviation **lb**. Libra is also a sign of the zodiac, symbolized by a scale and the only sign inanimately represented.

(The ancient Greek calendar, **zodiakos kylos**, or circles of figures, from **zodion**, a diminutive of **zoon**, meaning animal, and kylos, circle, graphically symbolized various constellations in an imaginary belt around the heavens. Zodiakos kylos was eventually shortened to simply zodiakos, hence our term **zodiac**. Why the inanimate scale joins the otherwise exclusive domain of animals is all Greek. It has been suggested that the balanced scales symbolize days and nights of equal duration during the autumnal equinox at the ecliptic.)

Our **librate** (from the Latin **librare**) means to oscillate slowly back and forth, seeking equilibrium like a scale. But for its "r" it's easily confused with **libation** . . . an intoxicating beverage. The **libationary** after consuming too much, may move side to side, striving for balance, but have no etymological connection with libration. However, the libational have a rather tenuous connection to another liber homonym. They could be reliving the ancient festival of **Liberalia,** an annual event honoring **Liber,** god of wine (and playmate of Baccus) and his wife **Libera.**

The **deliberator**, however, has much to do with libration. He weighs facts or alternatives in his cognitive scales before choosing a course of action. Another school claims the deliberator has much to do with liberation. Preceded by **de**, or the Latin down, the deliberator in this sense holds liberty in check while evaluating available options.

Interestingly, a **liberator** (from the Latin **liberare**, one who sets free) also **delivers**. The French frequently took the liberty of substituting a "v" for a "b" as Latin passed through their country on the way to England. One who delivers, hands over, as in a **livery** that rents out boats, cars or horses. The same sense applies intangibly in the Lord's Prayer supplication "Deliver me from evil," a morning-after thought of many a libationary. ❧

Eponyms

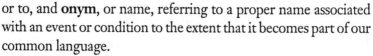

T HE MAVERICK, TRIED by **lynch law**, was strung from a sturdy branch, his frame **silhouetted** by the moonlight against a dense grove of trees.

The commonality among these bold face words is **eponymy**, from the Greek **ep-,** or to, and **onym**, or name, referring to a proper name associated with an event or condition to the extent that it becomes part of our common language.

A maverick, for example, can describe an unbranded steer or a politician swimming upstream against a cause not supported by his peers or electorate. The concept unwittingly was originated in the 1860s by a Texas rancher, Samuel A. Maverick. Unlike other cattlemen, Maverick refused to brand his cattle, his brand in effect being the lack of one. Legend has it that he vociferously complained when any of his cattle were missing, unrealistically hoping that his protestations and his cattle's lack of identification would trigger their return. Maverick thus became a term applied to anyone going their individualistic way.

Another famed eponym created about the same time, also a

legend involving Southwest cattle, is the **real McCoy**. According to this anecdote one Joseph McCoy, in the late 1860s, anticipated the opportunity of shipping cattle east via a newly constructed transcontinental railroad. Therefore he proclaimed that he would pay up to ten times the established rate for cattle driven up the Chisholm Trail from Texas to his cattle yard near the new transcontinental railroad line in Kansas. McCoy paid the inflated rate as promised, even though the head of cattle he shipped east grossly exceeded his own ambitious projections. Hence he was the real McCoy, as anyone can be who lives up to expectations.

(Another version, in the same time frame credits the A & M Mckay Company of Glasgow, Scotland, as the inspiration for the eponym. When its reputedly fine Scotch whiskey was imported to America, Scottish immigrants here attested to its quality as the real McCoy, pronounced with an "o" perhaps because a popular boxer named Kid McCoy was more established as a household word than Mckay.)

One could say for a while McCoy had his **doubting Thomases**, an eponym that goes back to St. Thomas, one of 12 apostles (the original disciples appointed by Jesus to preach the gospel). Per the Bible (John 20:25-29) he reserved judgment on the resurrection of Christ until Christ appeared before him, at which point Christ said, "Thomas, because thou hast seen me, thou hast believed; blessed are they that have not seen, and yet have believed."

More recent history is replete with eponyms involving unresurrected deaths. Consider **lynching**, or lynch law. Consensus credit for the term belongs to Captain William Lynch of Pittsylvania, Virginia, a town in 1780 without local courts to promptly administer justice.

According to the record, Lynch with his neighbors having "sustained great and intolerable losses by a set of lawless men," who "have hitherto escaped the civil power with impunity" were "determined to stop the iniquitous practices of those unlawful and abandoned wretches" and therefore decided to "inflict such corporal punishment on them, or him, as to us shall seem adequate to the crime committed or the damage sustained."

With that preamble and a conscious-mitigating strategy that could be termed cruel by today's standards, Lynch and his cohorts sprung into action. Per his words, "The person who it was supposed ought to suffer death was placed on a horse with his hands tied behind him and a rope about his neck which was fastened to the limb of a tree over his head. In this situation the person was left and when the horse in pursuit of food or any other cause moved from the position the unfortunate person was left suspended by the neck . . . this was called 'aiding the civil authority'."

Other sources also credit Charles Lynch, a justice of the peace and plantation owner, also of Virginia, for popularizing the eponym in the 1790s. According to legend he applied lynch law after growing weary of delayed justice for Tory supporters during our revolution.

The **derrick,** used for raising or lowering a boom, is of eponymic origin. Godfrey Derrick was a notorious 17th-century hangman who beheaded the condemned at the Tyburn Gallows in London with a hoisting apparatus that later bore his name. (Derrick's methodologies were not restricted to mechanical devices. The hangman's rope and the inhumane ax were among his tools of trade.)

Perhaps the most famous device associated with executions was misnamed. Again in the late 1700s, a physician and member of the French National Assembly, repulsed by barbaric hangings or sword beheadings, recommended that a mechanical device be utilized. He logically and passionately presented his case on the basis that the swifter process would be less painful.

The **louisette,** named after its inventor, Dr. Antoine Louis, became the new standard of execution. Thousands of Frenchmen in the French Revolution soon fell victim to its oblique blade, the most notable being King Louis XVI and his wife Marie Antoinette.

The Doctor (and assemblyman) most responsible for convincing his country to adopt the humane device was devastated when popular usage later decreed it in his name. After his death his descendants fervently attempted to change the eponym. Unsuccessful, they changed their name. No longer would any member of the family answer to the name of **Guillotin** (Joeseph Ignace Guillotin, 1738-1814), inspiration for the **guillotine**.

Another Frenchman who invaded our eponymic lexicon was a financier, Etienne de Silhouette, controller-general of France under Louis XV, in 1759. History leaves us with two possibilities explaining why his name became the noun for shadow outlines or portraits. His strategies for putting France's fiscal house in order by slashing expenses and raising taxes were extremely harsh and unpopular. The rationale underlying his methodology was judged shallow and insubstantial, like a shadow portrait. Another theory holds that **Silhouette** actually drew shadow portraits, attracted to the art form because it was so cheap. ⁊

Metaphors of the Sea

T OSS A LITERARY NET into the sea and you can pull in a **bouillabaisse** of metaphors and expressions. Delicious some of these morsels may be, but others inspire characterizations that are downright distasteful.

But first, bouillabaisse is deserving of a detour, so Thackeray advises us in his "Ballad of Bouillabaisse":

This bouillabaisse a noble dish is
A sort of soup, or broth, or brew
Or hotchpotch of all sorts of fishes
That Greenwich never could outdo:
Green herbs, red peppers, mussels, saffron,
Soles, onions, garlic, roach and dace;
All these you eat at Terre's Tavern,
In that one dish of bouillabaisse.

Etymologically, the dish's name tells more how it is cooked. It's from the French **boui-abaisso**, meaning, "Boil it, then lower the heat". . . **boui,** from **bouie,** to boil plus **abaissa,** to lower.

You could call this dish a **potpourri,** that is a mishmash of seafoods. However, this French term is a translation of the Spanish **olla podrida**: a pot of foul or decayed matter. Should the hostess responsible for this delicacy take you literally, you may be **ostracized** from her future social calendar.

In a more positive vein Shakespeare, in *The Merry Wives of Windsor*, reminds us we can strike profits anywhere, as one extracts pearls from oysters: "Why then the world's mine **oyster**/Which I with sword will open."

The Greeks took the I-E **ost**, bone, into their language as **osten** for bone and hard objects, and as **ostrakon** for oyster. In ancient Athens you could be banished from the area for up to five years if in a plebiscite enough citizens considered you a threat to the state. Athenians simply cast their votes by scratching the victims name on shell fragments, that is ostrakon, recycled as ballots, which were dropped in urns. Thus was born the concept of **ostracism.**

When thoughts of potpourri jumped a synapse, better you **clammed up,** as does the bivalve clam shut up. Both clam and **clamp** stem from the Germanic **klam-, klamb-,** meaning to squeeze together.

The idiom clamming up is positioned at the opposite end of the decibel range from **clamor,** a loud uproar. Clamor hails from the Anglo-French and Latin homonym **clam,** the equivalent of to claim, that is to assert, demand. It's ultimately from the Latin **clamare,** to cry out, understandable if unfortunately one's foot is clamped by a five-foot long Tridacna gigas, or giant clam.

A **clammy** handshake is how we often describe the other hand if it feels cold, moist. This modern sense is an outgrowth of the older sticky sense, related to the clamp and the clam.

That rich stew, **chowder,** like bouillabaisse, is named more for the means than the end. One legend claims Breton sailors, shipwrecked off the coast of Maine and desperate for food, cooked the ship's supply of crackers, salt pork and potatoes, along with locally gathered clams, in a **chaudiere,** French for kettle (from the Latin **caldaria,** a cauldron) and the source of our word chowder. The sailors gathered their clams only at low tide, thus explaining the expression, "**Happy as a clam at high tide.**"

Does the **lobster** escape this crustacean flight of illusion? Definitely not. English soldiers have been called lobsters. Like the cooked lobster they turned red, that is donned a red coat, upon enlisting.

If one suffers severely for not so severe reasons, **he dies for want of lobster sauce.** This expression has roots in a lavish feast given by the Great Conde (a French general) in honor of Louis XIV at Chantilly. Vatel, the head chef, learned that the lobsters required for a sauce had not arrived. (Quite possibly he turned red as a cooked lobster.) Unable to stomach his bitter disappointment and disgrace, Vatel promptly repaired to his room and committed suicide by the sword.

It's speculation, but the lobster probably owes its name to the spider, as its segmented body resembles the spider in an exaggerated form. Once he was known as a **lopister**, from the Old English **lopystre**. The latter, so the theory goes, is an alteration of **locusta**, Latin for lobster and **locust**, who leaps as does the lobster.

Definitely a more powerful swimmer is a vicious, terrifying, blood-thirsty killer, the **shark**, which cares less if it swallows prey dead or alive. It's ideally equipped to intensify our allusive references of the fish to swindlers and pilfers.

This hunter can hear sounds and smell blood a mile distant. A specialized layer of tissues over its eyes enhance its night-fighting capabilities by magnifying the faintest of light. Its powerful, 21-foot long body is torpedo-shaped for speed. Sharply serrated triangular teeth spread over a massive jaw enables it to open to a four-foot wide gap, leaving little doubt that this fish bites big.

Bertolt Brecht's "The Ballad of Mack the Knife" from *The Threepenny Opera*, capsulates our dread of the shark:

> *Oh, the shark has pretty teeth dear*
> *And he shows them pearly white . . .*
> *Just a jackknife has Macheath dear*
> *And he keeps it out of sight.*

Wise we don't mess with Mackie's girl; he may be back in town.

Nevertheless, a strong case exists that the shark is given a bum rap. Only four of more than 350 species are man-killers. And marine biologists warn us to cease our rate of shark slaughter. We can learn much from the shark. They have been around awhile. . .more than 400 million years. In comparison the dinosaur seems like a mere youngster, in existence for only 200 million years.

Wouldn't we like to capture the secret that explains why the shark rarely gets infections or develops tumors? Extracts from shark cartilage have also been used to treat human burn victims, and shark corneas have been transplanted to restore human eyesight.

It appears we are the rascals, killing sharks at a rate that will eventually cause their extinction. It's poetic justice then, that contrary to our crustacean examples, we named the fish after our own land-based sharks. English sailors first recorded sighting sharks in a 16th-century expedition to Africa and the West Indies. They named the fish shark, from the German **Schurke**, a rascal or greedy parasite, in turn from the Dutch **schurken**, to clutch, scratch, as do greedy parasites.

To **shirk**, another attribute of the greedy, first meant to live off others, then to escape one's responsibilities, and fittingly is a doublet of shark, having developed from the same root. Those who shirk also **sponge**, live like parasites, as does the marine animal sponge whose only mission in its sedentary life is to suck in water (up to 600 gallons in a single day) extracting all the bacterial fungi and plankton for nourishment.

If you think the sponge a tightwad, consider **barnacles**. They manufacture their own cement, secreted by a gland in their antennae, that adheres at a strength of up to 22 pounds per square inch. If their penchant for attaching themselves to boat hulls is ignored, they can cause a ship to not only lose speed but also to double its fuel consumption when operating at high speeds.

Undoubtedly his tenacity inspired Charles Dickens in his satire *Little Dorrit* to name a bungling and unqualified hanger-on official in the Circumlocution Office, Mr. Tite Barnacle.

And so it goes. One short and skinny calls to mind a slender shellfish, the **shrimp**. Without resolve or fortitude we run the risk of being compared to a **jelly fish,** as he is soft, spineless.

And that **crabby** guy with the bad disposition has been around since the late 1500s, the adjectival term germinated by predecessors like the sour tasting **crab apple** and the shell fish whose crooked, awkward amblings somehow were extended metaphorically to a perverse disposition.

When that metaphor, aphorism or expression is at the very tip of the tongue but will not come out, a glance to the ocean often will do the trick. "The tide never goes out so far, but it always comes in again," so the proverb goes. ❧

See "Kinky" for more oysters and crabs

Speaking of the Devil

B LASPHEMOUS TO MENTION God and the **devil** in the same breath? Heavens no, according to some speculative etymology. Old English for our devil was **deoful,** as was the Old High German **tiuful.** If we accept **deo** (a variant of the Latin **deus**) and **tiu** as God and **ful** a variant of fall, both words equate to "the god that fell" or perhaps "one who fell from the grace of God."

The devil and the Deity have long mixed it up in the Roman Catholic Church. In one corner we have the **advocatus diaboli,** the devil's advocate, and in the other, **promotor fideli,** defender of the faith, also known as advocatus Dei, God's advocate. With this adversarial arrangement, the advocatus diaboli sought to uncover any possible character defects or sins of a candidate for sainthood, while the defender passionately argued for canonization. Therefore in the extended sense we use the term devil's advocate to describe one who takes an opposing position to support an argument or examine an issue.

Cutting across many cultural boundaries is the predecessor of deoful: The Greek **diabolikos**, which also beget the French **diabolique**, Spanish **diablo** and English **diabolic** . . . all pertaining to the devilish, wicked or fiendish. This branch owes its ancestry to the Greek **diaballein**, meaning to slander, obviously a devilish act. Literally, diaballien means to throw (**ballien**) across (**dia**). Presumably, when slandering you throw, or cast, one's soul away. Whose soul? The "slanderee" may feel loss of soul through injustice. But a good Christian case can be made for the "slanderer" losing soul. He's denying truth, destroying his integrity.

The devil and his namesake Satan, has been generously tagged with euphemisms. Perhaps this explains the custom of referring to him in such expressions as, "what the dickens," "full of the old scratch," "the deuce," and the "evil one."

Nevertheless, he pervades our lexicon. The Scotch, in the 1700s, gave us **deil-ma-care**, implying that we really are reckless if the devil may care, but we do not. We knew long before our current enlightenment in nutritional matters that what tastes good may be bad for us, by naming **devil's food cake** (with its chocolate, butter, milk and whole eggs) the antithesis of angel food cake and its benign egg whites. We **give the devil his due** when approving an action of someone we dislike. We **raise the devil** when causing a commotion or vociferously staging a protest. And, of course, there may be **the devil to pay** if confronting an unwise or hazardous task.

Let the devil take the hindmost implies a penalty to a laggard. It's apparently based upon a superstition that the devil once ran a school in Spain. A condition of graduation was a ceremony requiring a run through an underground tunnel. The last runner in was the hindmost, and apprehended by the devil as his slave.

In a more narrative vein we are **between the devil and the deep blue sea** when presented with a dilemma of unattractive alternatives. This aphorism was begot from the Old French **diable,** used to describe the joints between various planks of a ship's hull that were awkward to caulk. To expose the planks for caulking the ship was beached at low tide. Hot pitch was lowered to sailors suspended from the ship's rail in boatswain's chairs. Two dilemmas were present. The caulking job had to be finished prior to the ensuing flood tide to preclude refloating an unseaworthy ship; and in haste, the sailors working feverishly to beat the sea's deadline were candidates for anointment with hot pitch. (The risk of a sail through the **devil's triangle,** the area roughly outlined by Bermuda, Puerto Rico, and Melbourne, Florida and famed for the demise of many sailing ships, would pale by comparison to the threat of a pail of hot pitch.)The sin of tobacco has been ascribed to Satan, per a limerick by Benjamin Waterhouse:

> *Tobacco is a filthy weed*
> *That from the devil does proceed*
> *It drains your purse, it burns your clothes,*
> *And makes a chimney of your nose.*

And he settles scores for our excess libations, as put by Robert Burns:

> *Wi' tippenny, we fear no evil;*
> *Wi' usquebae, we'll face the devil.*

This day and age few would recognize **usquebae** except by taste and scent. Like **whiskey,** its etymology leads us down a devilish path. We start with the water of life, **aqua vitae** in Latin, which many cultures somehow equated to distilled spirits, for example the similar sounded but compounded Scandinavian **akvavit,** a vodka flavored with caraway. The Irish-Gaelic preferred **uisga beathe** (from the Old Irish **uisce**, water plus **bethu**, life, a relative of the Greek **bios**). The Scotch, never silent over matters of liquor, weighed in with **usque baugh**, which with or without a slurred tongue, became **whiskybae** and finally their **whisky**, our whiskey.

The Russians have their **voda**, a guttural sounding aqua and of the same meaning. Its diminutive is **vodka**, implying that a little is precious, or perhaps that a little packs a big punch. And we get no argument from the French and their brandy, that is **eau-de-vie**, again water of life. Why distilled spirits, which can kill, are expressed as the water of life is left to our imagination. Any physical similarity is murky water at best. Perhaps we thought we could not face life without the stuff.

The face of the devil rises almost 3,900 feet and across the bay from San Francisco as **Mount Diablo**. Several legends suggest why the mountain received this accolade. One refers to a military expedition of Spanish soldiers from San Franciso that engaged the mountain's Bolgones Indians in 1806. As the tide of the battle swung in favor of the Indians, their medicine man suddenly appeared in full and startling plumage. Equating him with the spirit of the mountain and their defeat, the Spanish considered him **diabolical**.

Another tale concerns the relentless Spanish chasing Indian horse thieves, driving them up one of the mountain's steep canyons. The chase abruptly ended when flames gushed from a crater, the pursuers making a hasty retreat, pegging their prey as sons of the devilish mountain.

According to a *New York Times* account, a Catholic parishioner once addressed a group of clergymen at a saint's festival at the mountain, for the purpose of venerating the mountain. More loquacious than thoughtful, he suggested that the mountain be exalted, as many other California localities, by henceforth bearing the name San Diablo. The clergymen, having spent their lives **devil-dodging**, reacted in half-shock, half-laughter. The devil was never blessed with holy water; the request to spiritually bless Satan with sainthood was rejected outright.

Pressing the flesh

V ISUALIZE A RIOTOUS festival. Throw in flowers, sex, death and eventual rebirth, and you might have a scenario for a mystic orgy gone awry. Nothing could be further from the truth.

Though we may press the flesh at a festive **carnival**, in the original sense of carnival we avoided flesh. The ultimate sense of carnival is flesh farewell, or in Latin, **carnem** (flesh) plus **levare** (to raise, or to leave). Thus we didn't eat meat during Lenten fasting. However, human nature being what it is, merrymaking prevailed over sacrifice. Carnem and levare combined to form carnival to express the fun and revelry sense of a carnival during a period preceding Lent.

The fun culminates in Shrove Tuesday, or **Mardi Gras** literally fat (**gras** in French) Tuesday (their **Mardi**) which precedes Ash Wednesday, the day fasting begins. All this suggests one will be skinnier after Lent. And still more secular, a carnival today may stir visions of a travelling show, typically with merry-go-rounds, cotton candy and side shows.

Why Ash Wednesday? An ancient tradition decreed placing blessed ashes on the heads of parishioners while the priest proclaims " . . . for dust thou art, and unto dust shalt thou return."

It would be tough to get all this across to Fido, but that's why he's **carniverous**. . .carni, flesh, plus **vorous**,or devouring. And on a more somber note, **carnage** denotes a slaughter of a mass of humans, as in the tragedy of war, to be reunited with earth's dust.

Incongruously how does the beautiful **carnation** relate to all of this? The flower is named from its flesh-like tints. The palettes of Renaissance painters were awash in white, pink and light red hues. Hence **carnagione**, the Italian term for expressing flesh tones, especially a rosy complexion.

Since **carnal** pertains to flesh, it therefore extended to the body, in a sensual, seat-of-passions connotation, as opposed to the spiritual. History is replete with usage of carnal as a euphemism for sexual intercourse. The law once felt more comfortable speaking of **carnal knowledge**. Putting it in 13th-century phraseology we were "Blynded with sensualite and carnall pleasure." On the other hand one apparently repenting soul was told, "You haue forsaken your carnalnes, and begunne now to be spirituall."

Incarnate is investing with flesh. Hence Incarnation, in theological doctrine, refers to the embodiment of Jesus Christ in human flesh. **Reincarnation** applies to more common mortals. Any soul after death, under reincarnation, can be reborn and return to earth in another body. A handy term to know in the event you cherish visions of becoming a Baltimore O(o)riole your second time around, whether winging your way around the infield or tree tops. Sex, according to one wit (Henry Miller) is one of nine reasons for reincarnation . . . the other eight are unimportant. ❧

Getting Around

I MAGINE TRYING TO hail a cab during rush hour by shouting "**taximetercabriolet.**" By the time that mouthful is out your cab is halfway through the next block. Small wonder we have replaced that awkward compound with the abbreviated **taxi,** or simply cab.

The taxi part is from the Latin **taxare,** meaning to charge, as in any **tax** we pay. (Once taxes were extracted via labor, and thus were a **task,** or in French a **tache,** also a relative of tax.) Hence a **taxi dancer** is for hire at a price.

Taxi squad has nothing to do with charging, unless you're talking about one of the essential skills of a bruising lineman. This term came about because of the varied interests of Arthur McBride, the founder of the Cleveland Browns and owner of a taxi cab company. He maintained a group of reserve players, that by league rules could not suit up for games but nevertheless could stay in shape by practicing as unpaid team members, and thus be ready for activation in the event of injury to a regular team member. To circumvent the league pay restriction McBride paid them as employees of his cab company. Soon all pro football teams had their taxi squads, predecessor of today's development squad.

Rather straight-forward is **meter,** from the French **metre,** that is measure, as in computing our fare. Of richer heritage is **cabrio-let.** In 18th-century France it described a small horse-drawn vehicle and stems from **caprioler,** formed on the Latin **caper,** or goat. Just what is a goat's connection to our taxi? As the goat leaps it aptly describes a bouncing cabriolet. This suggests that both taxis and taxes are a pain in the rear.

If our driver slows to a comfortable speed, then abruptly accelerates, we could call his erratic behavior, thanks again to our goat, **capricious.** The word flows from the Italian **capriccioso,** which

originally denoted startled or frightened. It's a combination of **capo,** or head, as that of a goat, plus **ricco,** a hedgehog whose upright spines resemble hair standing on end, indicative of fright. Now usage has obsoleted the fear sense and translated the goat-like behavior to convey acting on a whim or impulse.

In an extended sense a frivolous or carefree action is a **caper.** And a free, irregular tempo of music may be deserving of the adjective **capriccioso.**

Taxidermy is not related to our taxi, unless you take the license that your jostling cab ride pops you out of your skin. Thank the Greeks for a convenient way of describing the task of preserving and mounting animals. Their **taxis** means arrangement (from **tassein,** that is to order or fix) and their **derma** skin.

Definitely smoother than a bouncing goat is a ride enjoyed in a **limousine.** Again definitely French, but for indefinite reasons. Limousine once was a term used to denote a long, flowing hood worn by shepherds of France's **Limousin** province. Unclear is whether the term later applied to the vehicle because its chauffeurs were cloaked in a shepherd's hood or because passenger and chauffeur were enclosed, that is cloaked in individual compartments. Further speculative fuel is added to the etymological fire since the inventor of the limousine, a Charles Jeantuad, hailed from Limousin. The luxurious aspect of limosine gives us **limousine-liberal,** a label for a wealthy politician that represents the working class.

Since the French named the limousine, it's fitting that they also coined its driver, the **chauffeur.** It's based upon their verb **chauffer,** meaning to warm or to heat, in turn from the Latin **calefacere,** composed of **facere,** to make, plus **calere,** warm. (Relatedly we have the verb **chafe,** to warm by rubbing, the **chafing** dish that keeps our food warm, and the **calorie,** a unit for measuring heat or energy use.) Early chauffeurs drove vehicles equipped with steam engines, similar to our Stanley Steamer. Therefore an essential duty of the chauffeur was to heat the boiler to generate sufficient steam prior to starting a trip.

Best not to travel by **cart**, especially in 17th-century England. Lawbreakers often were hauled around in carts for public chastisement and ridicule. "They will spitt at us and doom us Unto the post and cart," bemoaned one alledged evildoer in 1624. A death verdict resulted in a ride to the gallows in the executioner's cart, which left them dangling once the victim's neck was bound in a noose.

Cart is related to the Old Norse **kartr** and descends from the Old English **craet.** Although many car owners may consider their cars crates, **car** actually derives from the Latin **carrus,** or carriage. Its I-E predecessor was **kers,** meaning to run, then as in water and animals. The notion that a carpenter could make a car is absurd. Yet in a classical sense he does. Carpenter, related to car as a descendent of kers, derives from **carpentarius,** Latin for **carriage**-maker, in turn from **carpentum,** a carriage. Good carpentry, incidentally, was considered **harmonious,** not because the carpenter whistled while he worked, but because all the parts of his labors were considered **harmozein** (Greek) that is fit together, a term that hopefully applies to all the parts in your car.

The French borrowed words from the Greeks and the Romans to give us the **automobile:** From the Greeks, **autos,** meaning self, and from Latin **mobilis,** or movable, which together underscore self-propulsion as opposed to horse-drawn predecessors. For the first automobile, steam-engine driven, credit goes to the French inventor, Nicolas Cugnot, who in 1769 reportedly took the first automobile ride, at a roaring speed of 2.5 mph, and at the same time recording the world's first automobile accident by running into a tree. A German mechanical engineer, Karl Benz, probably deserves credit for inventing the forerunner of the gas-powered automobile. He did not hit a tree, but in his exuberance on a public trial run paid homage to Cugnot by hitting a brick wall.

As marketeers of cars remind us, autos come in numerous varieties. Take the **sedan**. Its origin is obscure, but it possibly stems from the Anglo-Saxon **sittan**, in turn the Latin **sedere**, both meaning sit. Gas consumption was of no concern. The sedan was first used for travel as a sedan chair. An enclosed seat suspended on two poles extending to the front and rear, enabled handlers to carry the sedan. The **coupe**, generally a smaller car, is a short version of the French **carrosse coupe**. . .carrosse being a coach, and coupe, a past participle of **coupper**, meaning to cut.

(Without the expansive concept of coup . . . a blow, strike, hit, thump, charge and numerous other actions . . . the French **coup de plume**, stroke of a pen, would indeed be a struggle. They accomplish a feat with one blow, **d 'un seul coup**, yet ward off blows or misfortune, **detourner le coup**, but can end one's misery with a **coup de grace**, a blow of mercy. Hardly anything escapes the force of the coup, including love . . . **coup de foudre**, literally a thunderbolt, is love at first sight; the state . . . a **coup d'etat** overthrows it; and the language . . . **coup de langue**, equates to slander, backbiting.)

If style is of no concern why not take "a mere ugly square box on wheels," as one Englishman described his nation's first **omnibus**. Now known by the diminutive **bus**, omnibus is ultimately from the Latin, **ibus**, indicating to or for, and **omnis**, or all. The English stole the word from the French **voiture omnibus**, that is vehicle for all.

Now in an expanded vehicular sense we have **busboys** to haul dishes for waiters and **busbars** in electronic components for transmitting signals and **omnibus bills**, catch-all legislation, typically involving numerous unrelated matters. Drivers of horse-pulled omnibuses displayed dedication to their jobs by riding the omnibus on their days off to verify that team and coach were properly treated by their replacement driver. Therefore, to this day, we use the term **busman's holiday** to characterize a vacation spent as one ordinarily works.

If you missed the bus, perhaps a **jitney** would appear. An almost obsolete term, it probably stems from the tax sense. In Jewish slang jitney means nickel, while the French **jeton** means token.

Obviously we can thank the French and the Romans for much of our vehicular terminology. Our Mediterranean friends, however, deserve credit for engineering roadways and relatedly discovering perils of traffic we have encountered in the 20th century. More than 50,000 miles of paved roads spanned the empire. We did not invent one-way streets, stop signs, parking on alternate sides of the street and traffic bans. It was the Romans. With their mounted horses and horse- and donkey-pulled carts Rome was stifled in grid lock in the first century AD. As a result personal hand-pulled carts were banned in congested areas during business hours.

All roads may have led to Rome, but without a more basic invention, the wheel, none of this mobility would have come about. Credit for the wheel belongs to the Sumerians of the Tigris-Euphrates Valley. Their unearthed tombs and pictographs reveal crude wagons and carts, vintage approximately 3500 BC. The wheels probably were a spin-off from the horizontal potter's wheel, which they enterprisingly tilted vertically for means of transport. We have been wheeling and dealing ever since. ❧

Old Soldiers Never Die: Eponyms II

C ONQUEST BY WORDS is more enduring than by swords. The Roman Empire prevailed for some 500 years, yet **Caesar**, its most famed leader, lives eponymously 2,000 years later, as the world's record holder for applications of his name. His surname, meaning emperor, invaded more cultures than he did.

For example, **kaiser** is the German version of Caesar, as is **keisari**, the Old Norse version. **Czar** or its variant **tsar**, is the Russian term for Caesar. Relatedly a czar's son is a **tsarevich**, his daughter, **tsarevna** and his wife **tsarvitsa**. We refer to a czar as one possessing absolute control, for example a czar of labor.

Erroneously Gaius Julius Caesar has been credited with the medical term **Caesarean** section, since he was born **a caeso matris utere**, meaning from the incised womb of his mother. **Caeso**, from **caesus**, the past participle of **caedere**, to cut, is related to the family name, which existed prior to Caesar's birth. Therefore, it's presumed that one of Caesar's ancestors similarly born was named for the procedure.

The name Caesar invaded our lexicon as **jersey**. An English channel island was named **Caesarea** to venerate the conquering general. Gradually its inhabitants changed the name to the Isle of Jersey. The island eventually became distinguished for its jersey cloth, which later applied to tight-fitting shirts or sweaters. Combatants on the gridiron, therefore, pay homage to the Roman warrior every time they don their numbered jersey. The island also became famed for the jersey breed of dairy cattle, distinguished for milk of high butterfat content.

Similarly **Nuova Caesarea** was once the name given to the area now encompassing the state of New Jersey. It was granted England's Sir George Carteret, the vice governor of the Isle of Jersey, in recognition of his support of the Crown in its losing battle to Cromwell during the English Civil War in the 1640s. (This also explains the existence of Carteret, New Jersey.)

Another city named in Caesar's honor is **Caesarea**, an ancient port in Israel, the Roman capital of Palestine when under Rome's occupation.

A mover and shaker, Caesar replaced the Roman calendar with the **Julian** calendar in 46 BC. In turn it was gradually replaced by sovereignties with the Gregorian calendar from the 16th century on, the Russians notoriously last to abandon Caesar's version. Playing with the calendar explains why the Russian "October Revolution" actually took place (Gregorianally) in November.

Caesar was not the only general to have his name remembered in eponymy. Several of the Union generals in our civil war are known more for their colorful contributions to our lexicon than their lackluster performance on the battle field.

Etymologists are slightly at odds over Major General Joseph Hooker (1814-79) and his ribald ways as the inspiration for **hooker** as a designation for a prostitute. Many soldiers of Hooker's division, located in Washington DC, frequented a popular red light district near Constitution Avenue. However, the term hooker for a prostitute predates the Civil War. No doubt Hooker and his boisterous troops popularized an existing term. Exactly how it started is left to speculation, possibly prostitutes snaring, or hooking, their prey on the streets.

General Ambrose Everett Burnside (1824-81) was fired as head of the Army of the Potomac in 1862 because of his failed campaign at Fredericksburg. However he achieved fame by cultivating a full set of side-whiskers that somehow in the reverse form of **side-burns** were named after him.

In contrast the confederate General Thomas Jonathan Jackson (1824-63) was regarded as an outstanding leader. When he was killed (1863) General Robert E. Lee observed, "I have lost my right arm." He received the nickname Stonewall by one of his officers who admired the general "standing like a stone wall" against the enemy during the Battle of Bull Run in 1861. Hence we now have **stonewallers** who persistently hold their ground against all opponents.

Even the winners lose at war. In the third century BC Pyrrhus, the king of Epirus in Greece, proclaimed after exceptionally costly victories over the Romans, "One more such victory and we are lost," hence the term **Pyrrhic victory.** Pyrrhus' perception was a self-fulfilling prophecy, his army later defeated and he was killed in a battle with the Romans at Agros in Greece.

Thanks to an innovative and distinguished French general we take soup and stew from a **tureen.** In the field and without a bowl for his soup Marshall General Vicomte de Turenne (1611-75) simply used his overturned helmet, so the story goes. As with Hooker, the French general's role in the eponym may be more of a popularization. Long before Turenne the French gave us **terrine,** an earthenware dish, in turn from the vulgar Latin **terrinus,** the Latin **terra** (earth).

You could wash all this down with **grog**, thanks to an English admiral, Edward (Old Grog) Vernon (1684-1757). Like our two Union generals, his career in the early 1700s, was not characterized by any brilliantly executed military campaigns. However, he is remembered for his **grogram** (from the French **gros grain**, that is large grain) a cloak of course material that he wore during periods of bad weather. Hence his moniker Old Grog. He's further remembered for ordering his sailor's rum diluted with water, thereafter disparagingly referred to as grog. Nevertheless, drink too much of the stuff and you are groggy! ⁂

Barnyard Justice

A JUDGE PROBABLY WOULDN'T take kindly to your comparing his **court** room to a barnyard full of cackling chickens, let alone identifying it as a hangout for bands of prostitutes. Yet history, etymologically, proves you right.

Court came into Middle English in varied French forms, including court, **curt** and **cort,** in turn from the Latin **cors,** a contraction of **cohort,** Latin for an enclosed yard, such as a garden. The **hort** of cohort gives us **horticulture,** hort (garden) plus **culture** (to cultivate, grow).

Cohort, itself, has been all over the lexical landscape. It originally enclosed a farm, and presumably because an army marches best on a full stomach, cohort became a division of a Roman legion consisting of three to six hundred soldiers. As soldiers and time marched on, the number qualifying for a cohort decidedly shrunk...to any group of soldiers, to a small gang that pulled off a robbery, to just you and your buddy who pulled in a big fish.

True, some cohorts may face judgment in court. Judicially we are in court, however, because a king upgraded the garden court to an enclosure for his castle and entourage. He also dispensed justice among his subjects within his court. Seeking justice you obviously would court his favor, or as usage later allowed, anyone's favor if you wanted one. Therefore we attribute **courtship** to wooing a potential spouse or to animal behavior prior to mating season.

"The pleassantest Part of a Man's Life is generally that which passes in Courtship,"observed an author in a traditional romantic vein in the early 1700s. An opposing view in the same time frame compared "Courtship to marriage, as a very witty prologue to a very dull Play."

Courtiers being in attendance at courts of royalty could hardly be expected to tell a king something he did not want to hear. They obviously exuded charm and became known as seekers of favors by flattery.

Royalty plays its court cards to the very end. A **cortege**, a derivative of cort, is a ceremonial procession of attendants and retinue associated with a funeral. **Courtly** or **courteous** (the Latin-based suffix **eous** meaning composed of or resembling) behavior when appearing in the king's residence is therefore respectful and noted for graciousness, a custom continued as downright practical in today's halls of justice. "Never underestimate the power of a simple **courtesy**. Your courtesy may not be returned or remembered, but discourtesy will," this bit of advice the courtesy of Princess Jackson Smith. Its most respectful and ceremonial form, the **curtsy**, is signified by bowing.

How did prostitutes appear where chickens once scratched? The French monarchy, for example, recognized that a king and his spouse represented a match not made in heaven, but in a political state, wherein a prince, perhaps an heir to a throne, was commanded to a particular marriage. His royal blood issue of princes and princesses became a pool of potential marital stock for later matches with royalty of other states. The arrangement enhanced diplomatic ties and provided levers of ambassadorial influence when needed.

With marriage grounded in the cold logic of international relations, small wonder kings cast lustful eyes elsewhere. Court mistresses, known by the euphemism of **courtesans** (or courteznas), therefore were not only accepted but encouraged. The euphemism was recognized long ago. "Your whore is for euery rascall, but your **Curtizan** is for your Courtier." ❧

Test-I-Ments

VIRILITY SHARES A common heritage with numerous odd bedfellows ... including the incongruent thought of castration, truth, abhorrent reaction to the Renaissance Popes, participation in competitive sports, presentation of evidence in court and the disposition of one's estate.

All this mishmash springs from the Latin **testis**, meaning witness, and in another sense, **testicle**. In ancient times man swore, or offered witness, to his word, by simultaneously placing a hand over his testicles. Perhaps he was signalling credence by analogously verifying something more important than his words–his virility. Another theory holds that the act solemnized agreement that his virility would vanish should his words prove false.

We may **detest** the perpetrator of false words, literally calling down (**de**) the wrath of the gods as a witness (**test**) against, or in wrath of, his unholiness.

This practice of signalling the truth obviously was sexist, but allows women to take the high ground: Always truthful, why do they need this bit of silliness?

Swearing by one's testicles appears in the Wycliffe Bible. The later King James version euphemistically cleaned up this act with references to placing one's hand over his thigh. (We don't swear off body part analogies easily when swearing to the truth. We are still known to place our hands over our hearts.)

The leap from virility to **castration** would seem imponderable if not for the lexicon of the Greeks. Testicle in Greek is **orchis**, presumably because an Athenian way back noted that the shape of a testicle resembled an orchid's tuber. Thus they gave us the medical term **orchidectomy** for castration (-**ectomy** meaning surgical removal).

When **testifying** in court we are literally making witness. . .testify, a compound of test plus the Latin **ficare**, to make. Proving that etymology is not an exact science, another more intriguing explanation advanced by some scholars hinges on testis flowing from **tristis**. In this scenario we have **tri**, as three, plus **stis**, a form of **stare**, the Latin verb to stand. Therefore our testifier, or witness, is a third party standing in **testimony** to a dispute of two litigants.

Testimony (test plus **monium**, the suffix indicating a condition) is ever present in the ecclesial. The ten commandments, per Exodus 31:18, were inscribed by "the fingers of God" in stone as tablets of testimony or evidence for judging human behavior. Titles of the two major portions of the Bible are translations from the Latin **Vetus** (old) and **Novum** (new) **Testamentum.**

The Lord at his Last Supper offered His testament, or last will, to his apostles. In that borrowed sense we make our last wills and testaments. One dies **testate**, having left a valid will, or **intestate**, without a witness to disposition of assets, relinquishing this determination to the state.

A **Protestant**, a Christian adherent not of the Roman Catholic or eastern faiths, actually owes his identification to the Latin **protestari, pro** (coming forth) plus (s)**tari** (stand) plus (test) as a witness, as did Luther's followers in breaking away from the Vatican. Somehow they did not regard some behavior of the Renaissance Popes as Christian, such as:

- Accepting payoffs in exchange for Papal appoint ments and pardons for those convicted of man slaughter (Innocent VIII).

- Bribing a competitor for the Papal throne with five mule-loads of bullion; supporting various mistresses and at least seven children; sponsor ing sexual orgies for the entertainment of his family and friends (Alexander VI).

- Riding as head of his army into war to contain Papal states (Julius II).

- Despite a shaky financial condition, holding lav ish dinner parties, culminating with the ritual of throwing gold plates out the window into the Tiber river; contriving and selling more than 2,000 offices during his reign to help support an extravagant life style; hiring an assassin to kill a cardinal that was tortured into a confes sion (possibly fabricated) that he planned to kill the Pope (Leo X).

As sure as the earth turned, a thirst for material treasures and power remained unquenched, as well as Papal taxation to foot the bill. No wonder the Lutherans eventually **attested** (**at** a form of **ad**, that is toward) their own sect and **contested** (**con**, against) Roman Catholicism. (And anyone competitively engaged, whether in sports or running for office, is a **contestant**.)

The tests you endured in school literally bore witness to your scholastic proficiency. Right? Wrong? If you answer right you fail this short test. The classroom test defies this bit of logic, coming instead from the Old English **teste**, formerly Old French **test** and ultimately the Latin **testa**. The latter was used to describe a brick, earthen pot or piece of fired clay. Testa, in turn flows from **tersta**, dry ground, hence the term **terra** for earth.

Our school sense of testing rose from the practice of heating an earthen pot, or cupel, to separate any impurities from an ore sam ple to test for residual gold or silver. **Putting it to the test** then expanded to all kinds of endeavors, including one's competence in the three Rs.

Related to our class room test are the tests of many inverte brates, such as sea urchins. They possess a shell, termed a test, since its hardness and shape resembles an earthen cup. ✍

Terms
of Business

L IKE THE BUSINESSES it describes, the lexicon of commerce
continuously expands... supply-side economics and junk bonds
representing just a few recent additions. However, some of the
older concepts of commerce, as prosaic as they may seem, possess
a rich heritage. Whether anxiously attending to personal business
affairs or details related to your employment, you are definitely **busy**.
Call business **bisines** (as did Middle English) or **bisignisse** (Old
English), it is a state of **(ness)** being busy, or **bysig,** an adjective in vogue
prior to the ninth century, meaning careful, anxious or occupied, all
essential qualities when engaged in business.

At home or the office we recognize the necessity of a **budget**
for estimating expenses. Our budget stems from the Old French
bougette, a diminutive of their **bouge,** a descendent of the Latin
bulga, a leather bag. A bag's connection to budget? Very simply,
Roman housewives set aside specific sums for major expenses, each
in their respective little leather bags, to assure that funds were available when payments became due.

True to tradition, England's Exchequer traditionally presented
the House Of Commons a written estimate of annual revenues
and expenditures, all stuffed in a leather bag, assuredly somewhat
bulkier than those kept by the Roman housewife.

With due diligence to the budget, we **purchase,** from the Old
French **pourchacier,** chase **(chacier)** plus forth **(pour).** In stark
contrast to the bewildering choices of consumer goods available
today and their hype of advertising and direct mail screaming for
our attention, nascent sales strategy several hundred years ago

involved at best a hawker standing adjacent to the entrance of a shop and announcing the identity of goods sold therein. It's understandable that a purchase was consummated literally in the spirit of a chase.

Who pays retail anymore? So, too, in the 1550s we bought at a **discount**, from the Italian slang **d'escompte**, the French **decompte**, later exported to England as discount. It originally referred to a practice of not counting, away (**dis**) from the **count**, a portion of the purchase as an incentive to the buyer. Therefore, our discount originally was a premium.

Why do we **shell out** for our purchases? One legend credits colonial America with the custom. Money was in short supply. Indian corn was coveted. Therefore many transactions were paid for in corn. But most purveyors demanded it be shelled.

If you think shelling corn an awkward **pecuniary** practice go back several thousand years. Cattle were the accepted media of exchange. Our pecuniary derives from the Latin **pecus**, their cattle, the I-E **peku**, equating to wealth or movable property. Relatedly, **peculiar** in the peku-wealth sense surfaced in the 15th century and referred to something belonging exclusively to an individual.

So revered was the cow that the first **coins,** appearing around 2000 BC, bore the images of cows as amulets or talismans to ward off evil and invite fortune to the holder. Coin is borrowed from the French, a descendent of the Latin **cuneus**, a wedge, which was used to stamp the coin.

Coins proved immensely convenient compared to leading around a 2,000 pound bull, but their eventual composition of rare metals and their value intrinsically equated to their weight, invited rampant counterfeiting. To test the validity of a coin one would drop it on a stone slab and judge its metallic composition from its tone† thus the origin of our expression to **ring true**.

(Ringing true, however, is in the ears of the believer. Metallic cups passed in European churches resonated with coins dropped through their slots. The faithful learned to discern the sound of a neighbor's 5, 10 or 50-centime piece or 1, 2 or 5-franc coin by the sound. When embarrassingly pressed for cash many a wily adolescent has been known to drop buttons, chosen for their content and size, to gild the acoustics with a respectable ring.)

Accumulate too many discordant coins and you were a candidate for **bankruptcy**, that is a ruptured bank. We can trace the word to an ancient German tribe, the Lombards, who settled in Northern Italy and engaged in money changing. They presided over an Italian **banca**, literally a bench, but one full of foreign coins. If one of them was robbed or miscalculated, the business became **banca rotta**, that is, his money bench was broken, as are we broke when out of money. Before the Italians got a hold of rotta the Romans gave us **ruptura**, to break, clearly a predecessor of the -rupt in bankruptcy.

The money changer's banca became the Middle French **banque**, our **bank**, a source of credit* that we often turn to when purchasing a home. Buying a house can be very exciting and rewarding. However, unless cash is paid the transaction basically is a **morbid** concept. Clearly the **mortgage** is a death pledge . . . from the Latin **mortus**, past participle of **mort**, to die, plus **gage**, French for pledge. Gage to a medieval knight was a pledge to fight, often symbolized by a glove thrown to the ground as a challenge to combat. We see a vestige of this custom in the WW II recruiting poster of a marine throwing his jacket to the ground, ready to fight the Axis.

What's not so clear is the rationale for the death element. One explanation holds that the debt dies only when paid in full. Another more intriguing anecdote hinges on the medieval promise of a strapped son to pay the debt from his inheritance upon the death of his affluent and noble father.

Every time we engage in a financial transaction we take a **calculated** risk, thanks to the Chinese and their **abacus**, an invention of the sixth century BC and still in use today. Abacus stems from the Greek **abax**, or slab. It was grooved to contain limestone pebbles, called **calculi** in Latin, and enabled users to calculate by positioning rows of pebbles, far preferable to crunching all those Roman numerals.

The algebraic **calculus,** definitely a higher form of mathematics than that performed with an abacus, like its relative the calculus pebble, stems from the Latin **calc**. So too, it is with **calcium,** found in limestone, and the derivation of what doctors call a **calculi** when referring to stony formations found in kidneys and gall bladders, as well as a **callus,** the hardened skin that forms on our feet.

Financially this brings us back full circle to the **callous** posture we are advised to assume when collecting a problem debt or letting go of a favorite stock when the management of a company becomes **calcified** and the firm's fundamentals show signs of deteriorating.

That's decidedly a bearish position. Why we are **bears** or **bulls** is a matter of conjecture. One could be characterized as bearing the load of a down market. Certainly many short sellers have a bear by the tail when their anticipated profits evaporate in a market that suddenly turns up. The more likely explanation is that they have sold the "bear skin before catching the bear," an allusion to the short seller's selling borrowed stock, and after it declines in price, buying it and profiting from the difference.

Bulls, on the other hand, want upward movement, a possible allusion to the animal's tossing things upward with its horns. Bulls also anticipate strong growth in their stocks. Our male cattle bull derives from the Old English **bula**, the I-E **bhel,** meaning to swell, strengthen, as does his pizzle, and hopefully your equities.

Of course, if the touted growth of a stock doesn't materialize, the broker's prediction proved all **bull**. . .this homonym from the Latin **bulla,** now our bubble, which in this case has decidedly burst. ❧

---

† See "Stretching a Point"

* See "From the Heart"

To Love Is to Win

IN LOVE, AS IN hunting and sports, winning is the name of the game. Call it **wen** (I-E), **van** (Sanskrit), **won, wen** or **wun** (various Germanic) and finally the Old English **winnan** and our **win,** it all meant to strive, thence to desire. But who wants to remember or aspire to losing? Thus desire evolved into a sense of winning.

To desire is also to love. Thank the Romans and their **veneris,** or desire (from Sanskrit van) for all kinds of etymological twists and turns down the path of love. From veneris we have **Venus,** the Roman goddess symbolizing physical love. In spiritual love we hold someone **venerable,** that is highly respected and honored . . . as, for example, the veneration of archdeacons in the Roman Catholic Church, an initial step in their canonization to sainthood.

Love can also be a no-win affair. One carelessly participating in the rites of Venus runs the risk of contracting **venereal,** or sex-related, diseases.

This affair with love gets far out when considering the planet **Venus,** the second planet in distance from the sun. (Mercury, the closest to the sun at 36 million miles, Venus is 67.2 and the earth 93.) It's also referred to as the morning or evening star, as it rises prior to, and sets after, the sun. Hence the rationale for folklore describing Venus's perpetual search for a mate, the sun god.

Proving again that usage refines and defines, our ancestral root of desire, wen, was extended to the I-E **wenesnom,** or love potion. Our term for the eternally sought love potion is aphrodisiac, eponymously named for the Greek's equivalent of Venus, **Aphrodite.** Wenesnom is the source of the later Latin **venenum,** a medicinal herb, now our **venom.** That, in the form of spite and malice, a jilted lover may hold against a former mate. Far better for the latter than the literal sting of a life-threatening **venomous** snake. Perhaps the blind aspects of love is what the Romans had in mind with their expression **in cauda venenum,** "in the tail is the poison." As with the scorpion, it's what you don't see at first that eventually hurts.

Perhaps further supporting that winning is the object in hunting and love, is the Latin verb **venari,** to hunt. It relates back to the basic sense of to desire or strive. It also gave us **venison,** which originally meant the flesh obtained from the hunt.

A hunter not bagging any game is certainly not with the spirit of wen, won or wun, in which case he may look to his mate for a **venial** understanding. From the Latin **venialis,** she would, thanks to Venus, be expressing a loving, pardonable forgiveness.

Venari is also the source of the almost obsolete English noun **venery,** a homonym that applies either to a sense of hunting or to the actions of one "given to fleshly wantonnesse." After all, observed Alphonse Kerr, "Love is a sport in which the hunter must contrive to have the quarry in pursuit." ❧

Pickiness Gets You Everywhere

P ICKING ONE'S TEETH may be considered gross. Nevertheless this bit of **pickiness,** among others, abounds and is downright intelligent. Take **leguminous,** for example. That's a mouthful. It's from the French **legumineux. . .eux** (that is **ous**) meaning of the nature of, plus the Latin **legumen,** referring to plants of podded seeds. Legumes underscore that we are a picky lot. They are so named, according to many etymologists, because seeds in a pod are easy pickings.

All this fastidiousness actually started with the I-E **leg**, to pick, choose, gather or collect, which became the Latin **legere** and its past participle **lect**, both of the same senses as leg plus the extended sense of reading. After all, reading is a process of picking out letters with our eyes (legere oculis) and rendering them **legible.** Spelling of the latter often is confused with **eligible,** a separate word but of common heritage. To be considered eligible, again, one must be picked.

The Latin **colligere,** the marriage of legere plus **col** (together) and its past participle **collectus** yielded the French **collector,** and ultimately our **collect.** Similarly, **eligere** and its past participle **electus** enables us to **elect** politicians. We are picking (lect) them out **(e).** Or, if we forget to vote, we are guilty of civic **neglect, ne** (not) plus lect (pick out).

A **negligee** (from the French negligee, in turn from the Latin **neglieger,** to neglect) derives from the fact that this loose gown is not gathered, **nee** (not) plus legere. On the part of our lady, its **selection. . .tion** (the act of) plus legere, plus **se** (apart) is hardly a matter of **negligence.** Rather her attentiveness to dressing for her mate, is a matter of **diligence, dil,** or dis (apart) as in carefully picking out something.

Indeed, her mate she hopes will regard her as **elegant. . .**that is in the modern sense of the word, refined, tasteful. It's from the Middle French elegant, in turn from the Latin **elegantem,** the present participle of **eligere,** which originally meant to be choosy . . . substantiating that to appear refined and tasteful one must pick her wardrobe with care. Odds are she knew of his **predilection** for her enticing attire . . . from the French predilection, in turn the Latin **prediligere,** or preference, a choice before **(pre)** other alternatives.

It would not be the preference of most Frenchman to become a **legionnaire,** a member of the French Foreign **Legion,** so named because the legionnaire is especially picked (again from the verb legere) for duty. Legere also gave us **legend,** originally a reference to tales picked for reading on selected church days, especially narrations of the lives of saints. Time often twists stories, which explains why enhanced exploits of the **legionary,** hardly saintly, may become **legendary.**

The Greeks took a slightly different spin to the I-E leg, transforming it into **legein,** with the same gathering, reading sense, which eventually referred to speech. According to etymological legend, legein likely yielded the Greek tools of speech, such as **lexis** (word) and **lexikos** (pertaining to words) and **lexikon** (wordbook) or our **lexicon,** as in dictionary.

By changing "e" to "o", and relatedly legein into **logos,** the Greeks literally have talked us to death and gave us all kinds of speech. . .a **monologue** for one; **dialogue,** involving two or more conversationalists; **prologue,** an introductory speech; and its opposite an **epilogue,** a concluding speech. They also gave us **apologos,** a story, and its derivative, **apologia,** a defensive story, from which we invoke **apology.** And, of course, their **eulogia,** speaking well (**eu**) denotes how we speak of the recently departed, as in our **eulogy†.** And supporting the metaphor that writers do occasionally blossom, an editor literally picks a bouquet of flowers when combining his choices for the most creative works. The ensuing **anthology** is born of the Greek **anthos,** flower, plus logo.

So far so **logical,** another logos word, which stems from the Latin **logica,** in turn the Greek **logikos,** meaning speech or reason. Similarly **logistics,** whether exercised in military operations or in the execution of a business plan, hinge upon logic. However, the word does not. It's from the French **logistique** (originally referring to the work of quartermasters) and literally a body of principles or facts, as represented in the suffix **istique,** from the Latin **ica,** the Greek **ika,** plus **log**(er) to lodge, in this case troops.

Logically, to write or speak, requires **intelligence,** once again legere (to discern, pick) plus **inte** (between or among) letters. Our

intelligentsia, a group of intellectuals, especially the social or political elite, came to us from the Russian **intelligentsiya,** by way of the French intelligentsia, in turn from the Latin **intelligentia.**

Whether or not you wish to be considered among the intelligentsia, picking your teeth of legumes is indeed an intelligent thing to do. Just ask your dentist. ᴫ

† See "Euphemistically Speaking"
* See "Raedan & Writan"

Circum Stantia

I F YOU OCCASIONALLY MISSPELL **stationary,** with the suffix **-ery,** you're not alone. The confusion has reigned for centuries. However, the seemingly disparate adjective and noun are actually kin. Stationery, the writing paper, originally was spelled stationary, and for very logical reasons. The modus operandi of sellers of writing materials and books was stationary, as they worked in a post, or standing place, from the Latin **stare,** to stand.

The literal **stationarius** distinguished the merchant from a wandering tradesman. Later, as Italians employed their term **stazioniere** for shopkeeper and as writers of Middle English used **stacyonere** to describe booksellers, the -ery suffix took on the figurative meaning applied to writing materials.

Later editors found standing a convenience. They adopted the third-person singular form of stare, or **stet,** to indicate a change of heart in their correction to a text and thus will stand upon the author's original wording.

When we got up from all fours and stood erect, the complexities we ushered into our lives were not confined to lower back pains. We, that is our I-E predecessors, called this process **sta**, a root in the form of "**st**" that eventually branched into the Latin stare, but also spawned an extensive array of English words. Just one of them, **stand**, can convey scores of senses, such as to **stand by, -for, -out, -pat, one's ground,** or **on one's two-feet.**

You can take a **stand** on an issue, an army can take a stand in battle, and both can stand a chance (as in expectation) to gain or lose. The standing sense of stare implies to occupy, as one does a room, per the Italian **stanza** (from stare by way of the Vulgar Latin **stantia**). Thus the figurative application of stanza to a section of a poem, which implies a stopping place or a pause.

Even a **prostitute**, whom on first blush one would associate with lying down, literally stands (**sti**) forth (**pro**). . .that is brazenly soliciting in public. Her services **cost**, also a relative of the stand family, from the Middle English **costen**, in turn the Old French **coster** and the Latin **costare**, to stand together, presumably because buyer and seller agree on the price. (It's also **understood**, that is to stand under or comprehend.)

Her price may depend upon **circumstances** (from the Latin **circum stantia**, that which stands around) or how busy she has been lately. If **destitute**, things standing away from her. . .(de) away plus (**statuere**) stand . . . she may not exhibit **obstinacy** about her customers bargaining . . . from **obstinatos** (**stin, stan**) stand plus (**ob**) against, that is stubbornly unyielding.

However, best in the era of AIDS to keep one's **distance** from her, that is stand away (**di**) and **resist**, stand back (**re**) from her temptations. Any envisioned **ecstasy** of this potential **one-night stand** may be short-lived. . .from the Greek **ekstasis** (**ek**) out of (**stasis**) stand, or out of place from where our emotions ordinarily stand.

Stare sired further confusion with its descendants **statuary**, a collection of **statues** (they stand, usually in public places) and **statutory** laws set up, that is **established** by legislatures as opposed to common law. Establish derives from Middle English **establissen,** in turn Middle French **establiss** and the Latin **stablire,** related to **stabilis,** or **stability,** or continuance of laws that a **constituency** may rely upon. Break those laws at the risk of **arrest,** another st word, from the stopping sense, possibly because when we first stood we stopped to visually take in our expanded horizon.

As **constituents,** together **(con)** we set up **(stitu)** a combining form of statuere or authorize others to represent us in legislatures or congress. We also can authorize a **constituent** assembly, one with power to change fundamental law, that is our **constitution.**

Your **status** is your condition, or **standing,** often related to your assets, or your **estate,** from the Middle French **estat.** In the political or social arena status relates to position and power. We cannot **state** with absolute authority, but chances are the political state glommed on to estate (a feat now well understood by taxpayers) and in the process absconded with the first "e."

Emerging **states** made a science of evaluating their status in terms of increasingly complex numerical data regarding revenues and expenditures. The Germans called this discipline **Statistik,** from the Latin **statisticum** (a course in state affairs) from the Italian **statista** (one skilled in statecraft) in turn from the Latin status. Now we evaluate the condition of all enterprises, public or private, with **statistics.** Those numbers being decidedly bearish may forecast **stagnant** operations, or in slang terms, a company **"going into the tank."** Both the adjective and the metaphor are relatives of our original sta, stare.

The tank came to us from Early English **stank,** from the French **estang,** in turn from the Latin **stagnum,** meaning a pool of standing, thus stagnant water, in **contrast** (stand against) to running water. Logic says that stank, that is the past tense of smell, like stagnant, also is derived from stare. The logic stinks. Stank is from Middle English **stinken,** Old English **stincan,** derived from the German verb stinken.

However, the military tank by appellation definitely is related to sta. When manufacturing its first fighting vehicles Great Britain cleverly marked the major components as if assemblies for water tanks, portable cisterns, in order to keep their production a secret. The code name prevailed. ✇

Behind Those Titles

CRATCH **ESQUIRE, WHICH** sometimes follows an attorney's name, and you may discover facts your barrister may not like. By definition the title bears no precise significance, other than self-proclaimed respect. However, per a British twist, designating oneself Esq. signals your status of a gentleman, but with the admission of your commoner background.

The word also once was used to describe an **escort**, probably equally unpalatable to your attorney in this day of escort as a code word for a partner-on-hire from a dating service. It came into Middle English in the 13th century from the Middle French **escuier**, from the Latin **scutarius**, a shield bearer, which brings us full circle to the protection we hope our attorney is capable of giving us.

Title we borrowed from the Latin **titulus**, an inscription or heading. Some etymologists speculate the Romans picked up title from the I-E **tel**, possibly their word for floor or board, hence the Latin titulus as a signboard, usually borne on the end of a staff or rod.

Interestingly, the lowest-ranking commissioned officer of the navy, the **ensign** literally bears a **sign**, (from the Latin **signare**, to mark with a sign). The pre-navy ensign was portrayed as carrying triumphantly a sign or banner suspended on a staff as a military standard to identify troops. We took the word from the French **enseigne**, in turn the Latin **insignia**.

Title boards are awash on the tops of desks, especially in banks. However, the holders thereof may be scarcely off the ground floor, especially **assistant vice presidents**. Vice implies a turning† sense that is in-place-of, while assistant from the Latin **assistere**, means to stand by, its **ste** a variant of **sta**, to stand*. All this relegates our assistant vice presidents to literally serve in place of, and stand by the real boss, and to thus bear their redundant titles not triumphantly. Even the office of the real boss can be one of quiet diplomacy, so observed George Bush, referring to the number of state funerals he attended as vice president in the Reagan term.

The turning, or in-place-of, sense of vice also is found in lieutenant. Whether a lieutenant commander or lieutenant general he literally holds a subsidiary role: **lieu**, French for in place of, plus **tenant**, from their **tenir‡**, to hold.

By virtue of vice, a **viceroy** is appointed to rule a country for a king, or **roi**, Old French for king; a **viscount** is a nobleman serving a count; and the ecclesiastical world is replete with deputies representing others, most notably the Pope, a **vicar** of Christ.

A title holder that leaves scant obscurity as to the source of his power is the **archduke**. A redundancy as to his claim to rule lies in part upon **arch-**, a combining form that indicates leader, ruler, possibly once emphasized by the threat of his **arku**, a bow and arrow**. And his leadership is underscored in **duke**, from the Old English **duc**, formerly the Old French and Middle Latin **dux**, which applied to one inheriting all this power. Dux, in turn, flowed from the Latin **ducere**, **duct-**, to lead. From this we **deduced** all kinds of things including, for example, **ductwork** which leads air through ventilating systems, and the **douche**, which **conducts** a stream of water for bathing.

We can add such disparities as an **education**, an act which hopefully leads students forward, perhaps equipping them to conduct a meaningful life. All this, however, does not preclude leading one astray from their principles, as may occur when **seducing,** that is **inducing** one into sexual intercourse.

The American navy's top boss, the **admiral,** owes his title to his occasional adversary of Middle Eastern waters. It's based upon the Arabic **amir-al-ma,** Arabic for chief (from their **emir**) of **(al)** the water **(ma),** which the Romans converted to **admirabilis,** and later **admiralis.** Admirablis is suspiciously close to **admirable,** a trait the flag officer may or may not have in the eyes of his sailors. It's high speculation, but some experts suggest the "d" found its way into the Germanic chief of the sea as a double play on the word to form the admire sense…that is for personnel on ships of the fleet to **(ad)** stare **(mirare)** at the admiral's lead ship for navigational guidance.

All in the military serve, especially **sergeants.** This backbone of many armies has defied an identity crisis despite its many variations . . . the British **serjeant,** Middle English forms **sergant, serjant,** and **serjaunt** as well as the Old French **sergent.** All this rose from the rank of the Latin **servient,** a participle of **servire,** equivalent to **servus** or **slave.**

Some in the army owe their titles to body parts. No argument that a **captain** is the head of his command. We inherited the title from the Middle English **capitain,** in turn borrowed from the Old French **capitaine,** which was derived from the Late Latin **capitaneus,** from their **caput** or head. This explains the slang expression caput, and the German **kaputt** for done, finished, ruined, as if the head had been severed.

Similarly the **corporal,** which heads a body of soldiers, takes his title from the French corporal, in turn the Italian **caporale,** also from caput. He doesn't administer corporal punishment. This corporal is a by-product of the Latin **corporalis,** of the body, and not surprisingly in a caput sense is related to corpse.

What could be less **private** than the private with the entire structure of the army bearing down upon him. Borrowed from the

Latin **privatus**, or apart, the word originally and derisively described someone without office, or in case of the soldier, without rank. This probably stems from England's custom of once contracting military missions to independent contractors that maintained ships and private soldiers, both known as **privateers**.

Though ranking far above a private, a colonel's etymology is hardly less disparaging. The rank derives from the Italian version, a **colonnello**, based upon the Latin **colonna**, whence the English **column**, not because of his upright bearing, but because he led a column of soldiers.

As the rank migrated to France, colonello suffered a dissimilation of its two awkward "l" elements resulting in the French **coronel**. Still not satisfied, the French contrived **colonnel**, a reversion to two "ls" and a bewildering word to pronounce and spell, which explains our English **colonel** and its pronunciation as "kurnal."

The ultimate boss derives his authority from dual etymologies. As **commander-in-chief** he issues written orders. . .from the Latin **mandare: manus**, Latin for hand plus **dare**, to give. . .all intensified by **com**, together. **Chief** underscores that he is the head mandator. . .from the Anglo-French chief, in turn the Old French **chef**, based upon the vulgar Latin **capum**, a variant of **caput**. (Thus a chef is the chief, or head, cook.) On the other hand, the commander-in-chief is also the **president**. As such he **presides**, or sits (**sedere**) forth (**pre**) . . . that is occupies the seat of authority.

He is often at odds with **senators**, who probably hold the record for titles that belie the office. The I-Es gave us **sen** for old, eventually transformed by the Romans into **senatus**, a council of elders. Sen also yielded the Latin **senilis**, our **senile**, a characterization many constituents hold for their senators. &

† See ". . . And Turning"
* See "Circum Stantia"
‡ See "Stretching A Point"
** See "Ships of State"

Raedan an' Writan

EVER BEEN TOLD YOUR handwriting resembles chicken scratches? Take heart. You're true to the very basis of **writing**, from the Old Saxon **writan**, to tear, scratch and later write. As a **scribe** … from the Latin **scribere**, in turn the I-E **skribh** … your writing, or **script**, is an etymological throwback to scratching, first pictographic symbols, then letters, syllables and finally words, into the bark of a tree and eventually clay tablets. Along the way we developed an **alphabetos**, cleverly labeled so by the Greeks, who knew their ABCs, from the first two letters of their alphabet … **alpha** plus **beta.**

English often presents several ways to express a singular thought. Surprisingly, so did I-E. Its skribh was duplicated in their **gerbh**, later picked up by the Greeks as their **graphein**, to scratch; **gamma**, letter; and **grammatike**, pertaining to writing or literature.

And let's not overlook **paragraph**. The Greeks were the first to offer readers graphic visual relief from the traditional, solid and often intimidating pages of manuscript by inserting horizontal marks at logical subject breaks. Their term for these breaks is a **paragraphos**, by the side of (**para**) plus **graphos**, or written.

The combining form -graph explains a family of our communicative terms, including **telegraph, tele** meaning distant from the Greek tele, far; **autograph, auto** equaling self; **grammar** schools, originally concerned mostly with Latin; and **graffito**, an Italian way of describing drawings, usually done after school. Concerns over **graffiti** go back a long way, per the Latin **stultorum calami carbones moenia chartae**: Chalk the pen of fools, walls (their) paper.

The Greek's graphein also sired **graphite,** a soft, carbon mineral that puts lead in our pencils. **Pencil,** earlier our **pinsel,** came to us via the Roman's **penicillus,** an artist's paint brush. If you think this has something to do with **penicillin,** you are absolutely right. The tufted or brush-like appearance of Penicillium mold inspired the name for the antibiotic. The similarity to pencil of another common writing instrument, the **pen,** is coincidental. It owes its heritage to the Latin **penna,** a feather, as our first pens were fashioned from quills.

The Romans' answer to the Greek grammatike was **grammatica** and denoted more than writing. It included a broader spectrum of astrology and magic. And, why not? After all, writers were viewed in some quarters as gifted with magical powers. The Scots had a say in all of this, respelling the English grammar as **glamour** with its usage tilted more toward the magic. Magically, they gave the word back to the English who picked it up as a sense of alluring, fascinating... a characterization many a fiction writer hopes a critic will ascribe to his or her writing.

In a contradiction of terms history was long recorded before historical records. In his *A Search for Scotland*, R.F. Mackenzie loved to point out to his pupils the **scarified inscriptions** left by water and ice on his beloved countryside and connect the physical characteristics of the valleys and terrain to the people who dwelled there . . . the rock from which we are hewn.

The ocean wields the mightiest pen of all. Ceaselessly pounding the shore, its waves carve inlets that are eventually bordered with buttresses left jetting out to sea. Later they poke caves into the buttresses, finally culminating in a tunnel. Continuous **scratching, scarifying** eventually collapses the roof of the cave, leaving a string of angular, isolated sea stacks to defiantly withstand the ocean's creativity.

Early scribes, almost exclusively members of the ecclesiastical, produced **manuscripts (manu)** by hand, or **Scriptures** when considered sacred, in shrines, established to protect their works and writing materials. Candidates for enshrinement have decidedly changed, as for example, professional ball players and their Halls of Fame, write or not.

So revered were the talents of scribes that ecclesial law of the church forbade **proscribing** the death penalty for a member of the clergy, regardless of the heinousness of a crime. Under "benefit of clergy" members of the church, from clerks on up, escaped capital punishment when proving their ability to read by picking out[†] specified verses from the Bible.

One traditional verse was Psalm 51, fittingly, "Have mercy upon me, O God," for ample reason to become known in slang as the "neck verse." If read correctly in Latin, the court's chaplain would pronounce "Legit ut clericus" (he reads like a clergyman) and the accused's life thus was spared.

Undoubtedly "benefit of clergy" was a great boon to church affiliation, attracting many a knave. As ecclesial courts bowed in favor of civil authorities, this loophole, sometimes exploited by ostensible candidates for the priesthood, fell into disuse. However, benefit of clergy was upheld into the 17th century and not wiped off the ecclesiastical books until the 18th century.

Proscription, the act of setting forth in law, is exactly what England had in mind after Scotland became absorbed in the British Empire following bitter centuries of continual military struggles. Many rules ensued to tear the fabric of Scottish culture, one of the more resentful prohibiting the wearing of a kilt, which ironically fomented patriotism. (By Sir Walter Scott's time the ban was repealed. Even the obese King George IV on a state visit to Edinburgh was convinced to wear a kilt over his silk tights after a bit of persuasive conversation and the best of sipping Scotch, both plied by the loquacious Sir Walter Scott, and thus eliciting a rather massive yet royal approval for the revered dress.)

Scribe begat numerous compounds including **conscript**. A conscript doesn't have to be a writer, but his name literally is **inscribed** together (**con**) with others on a draft list for military service. The tradition dates back to Roman times. Best be **nondescript**.

Scribere also gave us a derivative **scribble**, almost meaningless, indecipherable scrawls, which leads us to **prescription**, as most pharmacists and laymen alike will attest, when trying to decipher a doctor's orders.

As scribes have their scribbles, so **readers** have their **riddles**. The Old English **raedan** conveyed a sense of putting things together, thus giving advice or interpreting what puzzles or riddles another. Indeed, we were solving riddles long before we solved the riddle of reading. The seemingly inappropriate response, "I don't read you," to spoken words, makes sense after all. ❧

† See "Pickiness Will Get You Everywhere"

One Word Generates Another

W ORDS, LIKE THOSE WHO bespeak them, beget. Particularly proliferate is **gen**, the I-E root meaning to give birth. Its **progeny** are characterized by varied hereditary senses, ranging from the subtle to the extreme.

Generate, that is to produce, for example, traces its ultimate ancestry to gen, via its more immediate **progenitor**, the Latin **generare**, to beget. The same sense of producing is contained in **oxygen**, because some French chemists in the 1700s suspected that this gas that prevails in about a fifth of our atmosphere, when combined with other elements, was an acid-producer. Thus they combined the Greek **oxys**, meaning acidic or sharp, with the producing sense of gen.

The Greeks have been playful with **oxy**. Mated with their **moros**, foolish or dull, we have an **oxymoron**, a self-contradicting figure of speech, as is something sharp yet dull. That's why we have **sophomores**, students wise (the Greek **sophos**) yet dull like morons, as they are only partially schooled. They engaged in **sophism**, from the Greek **sophisma**, cleverly and deceptively arguing their points of view regardless of the underlying truth. This **engenders** visions of a modern trial lawyer's tactics: To win is in. To seek the true, no longer they pursue.

Relatedly, the **sophisticated**, no longer naive or **genuine**, instead are worldly-wise. There's a sense here of artificiality, impureness, as exemplified by a slick PR campaign of an oil-producing polluter extolling virtues of its corporate citizenry.

In the classical sense sophisticates are **adulterated** . . . to **(ad)** plus **alter** (**ulter,** when combined with ad). Thus **adultery** describes an illicit or impure relationship. This brings us full circle back to gen, as an adulterous relationship is characterized in some circles as **degenerative**, a falling away (**de**) from an ancestral standard of one's race (**gener, genus,** or race one is born into).

Whether race, tribe or family, membership therein can be characterized as of the same **kind**. Kind, **kin, kindred,** and **akin** are all kin. Replace the "g" of the I-E gen with a "k" or a "c," as did the Common Germanic tongues (that bridged the I-E with the German, English, Dutch, and Scandinavian) then play with the vowel and we have all kinds of kin: Old High German **kunni,** Old English **cynn,** and Old Norse **kyn,** to name a few.

Kindred is a story itself. From the Middle English **kinrede, kynrede,** it's a marriage of kin plus **raeden, raedan**[†] to advise or read, a tradition among family members. Can the knee, from the Latin **genu,** claim a birthright to the gen family? After all, per an ancient custom, the father of a newborn held his progeny on his knee to proclaim the child genuine. Most etymologists claim proponents of this theory are a little **generous** with their semantics, and relegate it to folk etymology.

All this brings us to our kind, that is children. Give them a garden to play in, as did the Germans (their **Garten**) and we have that delightful term for the beginning of school years, **kindergarten**. We're kind to kin. But not always, as Shakespeare's Hamlet reminded us when he spoke of his uncle as "a little more than kin, and less than kind."

With kind in mind, we can visualize **gentiles** as of the other kind or race, as the Jews regard Christians or the Mormons do anyone not of their kind. Thus the expression also can designate a heathen, which undoubtedly would elicit an argument from a Jewish resident of Utah.

Our ancestral gens is almost **generic** to our concepts of creating life. We term the reproductive organs **genitalia**. Being **pregnant** is literally a pre-birth condition (**gnat,** derived from the Latin **gignere,** to beget). It doesn't take a **genius** to realize that the **Genesis** book of the Bible pertains to the Creation. Our geniuses are so, because once we thought that their birth was attended with a guiding spirit, **engendering** them with special talents. **Geneticists**, however, tell us that the **genes** we inherit determine our hereditary traits.

As an **engine**, gen drives concepts beyond the biological. Those born with natural talents may become **engineers**, and cleverly create all kinds of mechanical things, including, you guessed it, the engine, considered an **ingenious** contrivance, as was the cotton **gin.**

The birthright of gen was a literary license to ramble. Change the suffix of ingenious, as in **ingenue**, and you're describing an innocent, naive, artless young girl, because that's her native, or inborn, character. One possesses a **gentle** or mild-mannered character, on the other hand, because of noble birth. The well-born male is entitled to a coat of arms, the herald symbols, for example, worn by medieval knights over their armor. All this seems rather incongruous to the mild, meek, and non-belligerent nature of a gentle person.

A **gendarme** . . . from **gens d'armes,** people at arms . . . may be a **gentleman.** But don't call him gentle. Though your intended characterization may be **benign** (of good nature) our warrior would probably feel **maligned.**

† See "Raedan & Writan"

Barbs We Know

HOW CAN **BARBARIANS** WITH their implicit savagenes and cruelty, bear any connection with babies, characterized with innocence and universally deserving of utmost tenderness? Beyond the fact that both are uneducated and that even a barbarian was once someone's baby, the connection is far from ludicrous. Chalk it up to the "ding-dong", also known as the "sing-song", theory of language development.

First, a bit of wordy lineage. Our barbarian descended from the Latin **barbaria,** meaning a foreign country. Relatedly, the Latin **balbus,** refers to stuttering or stammering. The Romans picked this up from the Greek **barbaros,** the latter's way of referring to someone who didn't speak Greek, or who was a **babbling** foreigner.

Now comes the real clue. The Greeks fashioned their barbaros from the I-E root **baba,** their expression for baby. According to sing-song theory, which holds that some words developed in an imitative or echoic manner, the ba-ba-bar sounds of baby could explain the I-E baba and reminded successive cultures of how a foreigner sounds with his unintelligible, stammering, stuttering **babble**. So fitting then that since Shakespeare, stage directors have coached players to repetitively utter **rhu-bar-bar** when projecting a crowd scene of all talking in the background without intelligible words.

Also connotative of confusing language is **Babelise**, derived from the ancient city of **Babel**, or **Babylon**. There, according to Genesis 11:7, people attempted building a tower to heaven, but confusion reigned with all the languages spoken. Interestingly, Babylon actually was located in Mesopotamia, between the Euphrates and Tigris rivers, near Iraq, within the boundaries, some scholars speculate, of our I-E linguistic heritage.

Consider the following babble, all meaning barbarian, and substantiating the common I-E ancestry of the many Germanic languages: **barbaras**, Sanskrit; **babbelen**, German; **babbla**, Icelandic; **barbare**, French; and the Spanish **barbaro**, to name a few.

Roman invaders of Africa's North Coast called the natives **barbari**, as did later invading Arabs call them **al-Barbar** . . . hence the area stretching from Egypt to the Atlantic is known as the **Barbary Coast**. The Arabic barbar was transformed to **Berber**, the name for North African tribes, living in the Barbary Coast and in the Sahara.

In the late 1700s barbarians there coerced protection money from the United States to protect its ships from pirates. Thomas Jefferson, when elected president, refused to acquiesce to this extortion and war ensued with Tripoli (now part of Libya) and later Algeria.

The oldest, fully commissioned warship in the world, the US Constitution, still part of the US Navy (berthed in Boston) played a major role in successfully ending Tripoli's reign of extortion by blockading the port of Tripoli and bombarding its fortifications and gunboats.

The gambling, prostitution and drinking associated with the Gold Rush ascendency of San Francisco in the mid-1800s was apparently looked upon as **barbaric** by some, thus the appellation Barbary Coast for the city's water-front district.

If your name is **Barbara**, do you have anything to do with barbarians? Yes, but don't despair. Foreigners took on an exotic sense. And in that spirit the Greeks invented the female name, Barbara.

All this is a close shave from our local **barber**. He comes to us from the Old French **barbeor**, from **barbe**, in turn the Latin **barba** and ultimately the I-E **bhardha**, all meaning beard, which the barber shaves. **Tondere** to the Romans was to shave, hence their **tonsura**, a shearing, and later the brief reign of the elegant term **tonsorial parlors** during the Victorian age. **Barbados**, the island in the British West Indies, probably was so named by Spanish or Portuguese sailors, impressed by the bearded appearance of the exposed roots of local fig trees.

Was Adoph Hitler castigating Russians as barbarians by invoking the code name **Barbarossa** for Germany's WW I invasion of the USSR? Absolutely not. He was invoking the memory of Frederick I, also known as Barbarossa, Red (**rossa**) **beard**, who became King of Germany (1152) and later the Holy Roman Emperor. Revered as a military hero, he became a legend after his death from drowning while crossing a river during the Third Crusade. So goes the story Barbarossa is asleep in the Kyffhauser Mountains, his beard still growing, and ready to be awakened to save Germany from its enemies.

If not the word, the thought of our original barbers smack of **barbarism**. They were general practitioners, providing services of shaving beards, cutting hair, bloodletting, extracting teeth and general all around surgery. It took a long time for surgeons to forge an identity separate from barbers . . . something we don't want to contemplate while on the gurney in route down the hall to surgery. It was a bloody business, exemplified by the blood-soaked rags tied around a white pole to dry, probably the same pole you gripped during surgery in a vain effort to fend off the pain. Some undergoing surgery did not survive, unlike the red and white pole that ornaments virtually all barber shops. ❧

Twisting

CURRENT COMMUNICATIONS vernacular for slanting a story is to put a spin on it. Not an inappropriate word when you consider we have been spinning yarns for centuries. But the longevity record for all this veering around lies with **twist**, as the Romans and the I-Es told us centuries ago.

A **torch** can shed some light on this. It can be traced back to the Old French **torche**, the vulgar Latin **torca**, something twisted, from **torquere**, to twist, and ultimately to the I-E **terkw** of the same meaning. What the Romans twisted to give us a torch was tow, that is fibers of flax dipped in wax, which when lit, lit their way. It took a while to break the torch habit: Early flashlights were known to the British as electrical torches.

Now we have twisted the usage of torch any number of ways. We pass a guiding torch to those who follow us, as John Kennedy reminded us in his famed inaugural address in 1961: "Let the word go forth from this time and place, to friend and foe alike, that the torch has been passed to a new generation of Americans . . ."

We can carry a torch and possibly **torment** over the object of our love whether reciprocal or not, per T.S. Eliot's poem "Ash Wednesday":

Terminate torment
Of love unsatisfied
The greater torment
Of love satisfied.

Just what has torment to do with this? Its progenitor was the Latin **tormentum,** which was chopped by the English to **torment,** a machine of **torture** which worked on a **twisting** or **torsion** principal, as did the torture by painfully twisting a victims limbs.

A twisting of rightful behavior into that wrongful is a **tort.** A California liquor store owner claimed that our tort liability laws have been twisted out of shape and that overdue reform has been moving slower than a **tortoise.** A prowler when attempting to break into his store after hours fell through the skylight, was injured and sued for damages. After all, a responsible store owner should have skylights capable of supporting crooks. The owner's **retort** (a twist back) was full of expletives and a costly court date was in the offing. He viewed his subsequent agreement to settle out of court for $5,000 as a payment **extorted** (twisted out, of him) and justice **distorted** (twisted away).

The tortoise, a land-based turtle, doesn't move very fast. Why hurry? Some have been known to live for two centuries. One look at his feet though offers a clue why he's a tortoise. They are crooked, yes, twisted.

We twist things as well as ideas out of shape, including the meaning of twist. At one time the Middle English **twisten,** meant to divide, to disagree, as were several tongues over its meaning. The English and Dutch, held twisten to a sense of division, disagreement. But the Flemish twisted its sense into **entwine.** All, though, were in agreement that fibers or hair were divided prior to entwining or braiding. The second step of this dividing-entwining process prevailed. Thus we twist fiber to make twine.

Back to our tortoise and his **tormentors.** Sailors long ago learned of an easy way to keep fresh meat for dinner as near as the deck along side the galley. No need to lash the poor turtle. Simply turning him on his back rendered him helpless, as it is impossible for the turtle to move or right himself from that lethal position. This all explains why when we **turn turtle** we are caught in a situation without a perceived solution.

The chap that inspired our term **turncoat** for a double agent or one of changing national loyalties certainly was no turtle. Unsubstantiated folklore credits several dukes, operating between France and Spain as well as France and Italy, for the term. A reversible coat, colored to represent one country on one side and another country on the other side, did the trick. The duke simply exposed the color of the country of his current choice. ⟨⟩

... And Turning

VERSES OF POETS INSPIRE us. But what inspired us to conceive the term verse to describe a line of words with a metrical ring? Incredulously we turn to the farmer. As a poet ends a line of verse (from the Latin **versus**, from **vertere**, to turn) he turns back to begin another, figuratively mimicking the plowman with his oxen when turning to trench another **furrow.**

Interestingly, a furrow in Old English farming measured a **furlang**, a telescoping of a furrow long, or 220 yards, now known as a **furlong.** The ridge created between the furrows was termed a **porca** by the Romans, based upon the I-E **perk, pork**, to dig. **Perky** in the English sense our farmer was not, if it took him 220 yards to compose a line of verse.

To be perky, a variant of the Middle English **perken,** one must rise jauntily, as does the bird when **perching** by lively alighting on high to be aware of all going on. Our perk, that is being lively, rising smartly, probably stems from **peer,** to discern, come into view, a variant of **appear,** from **apparere** in Latin, that is **parere** (be visible) plus **ap,** a variant of **ad** (toward).

Can we escape this sense of turning by turning to **prose?** Absolutely not. It's from the Middle French and Latin **prosa,** meaning factual speech, from the Latin **prorsus,** a contraction of **proversus,** the past participle of **provertere,** meaning to turn forward **(pro)** . . . proving that its etymology is hardly straightforward.

Therefore prose is not verse, and **vice versa,** a term that seems redundant. Vice, stemming from the Latin **vicis,** means instead of, and versa, the feminine, singular form of versus, the past participle of vertere, means turn. Thus vice versa turns an occasion, event and many a title around. The turning sense of a **vice** president, for example, lies in the VP substituting for the president.[†]

Vice holders more **versatile,** from the Latin **versatilis** or turning, are capable of turning to many disciplines and thus are candidates for the top job. Once appointed the thrill of holding the top spot is no longer **vicarious,** that is second-hand or imagined, again from the Latin vicis.

We suffer from many homonymic vices . . . from the Greek **homos,** or same, plus **nym,** a contraction of **onyma,** name. They are spelled identically but are of different derivations. Vices, the kind that a Frenchman defined as those that give up on us and thus we flatter ourselves that we are giving them up, stem from the Anglo-French, Old French and Latin **vitium,** meaning fault. **Vise,** also spelled **vice,** the clamping tool, which opens and closes through the mechanics of a screw, came to us from the Old French **vis,** or screw. Vis owes its heredity to the Latin **vitis,** or vine, inspired by the latter's spiraling tendrils.

Once appointed a chief executive officer our former VP must turn to many problems, employees and "publics". At times best he be an **extrovert**, turned outward. When turning over heavy decisions, however, the buck stops with him and, therefore, at times of deliberation he can be characterized by his associates as **introverted**. Definitely shunned as a candidate for the top is one **perverted**. He'll turn away from the expected course, render false judgment and eventually be **subverted** by his board of directors.

Prose designed to capture our discretionary purchasing dollars is displayed by way of **advertisements**, often scrunched into **ad**. The latter also serves as a prefix meaning toward, denoting in the advertisement sense whence our attention is turned. A **controversial** ad (turned plus against, **contra**) may irritate its audience in an **adverse** manner, casting its sponsor into an unfavorable perception.

This adds up to the obvious clue into the original sense of an advertisement, ironically a cousin to **adversity**. They were issued as warnings (the French **avertir** means to warn) possibly concerning an approaching **adversary**, a thought worth recalling when sorting through junk mail advertisements chronicling get-rich-quick schemes.

Churning these turnings raises the question whence the word **turn**. We have been turning since birth, perhaps before as indicated by the turned fetal position. Our turn traces its lineage to the Old English **turnian**, **tyrnan**, from the Latin **tornare**, the Roman's verb for turning objects on a lathe, obviously foot-powered, thanks to the Greeks and their **tornos**, a tool for chiselling circular objects.

This brings us full circle to more cerebral applications spun from this marvelous tool. Such is the Latin and Middle French borrowed **tornus**, which later inspired our **tour**, usually a product of many turns, as many a traveler attests.

It's scarcely a **detour** to appreciate why when faced with a problem often we engage an **attorney**. His appellation hails from the Anglo-French **attourne**, one who is turned to. One domestic matter that usually requires an attorney's counsel, and qualifies as a major turning point in life, is a **divorce,** that point in life when one realizes, so advises John Fuller, "Better a tooth out than always aching". Divorce is from the Anglo-French and Latin **divortium,** a variant of **divertere,** to **divert,** equivalent to **di** (divide) plus vertere, a redundancy that hardly leaves room for any ambiguity.

We turn to lawyers for their **advice.** On the surface, it seems to me, an obvious case of turning toward (**ad**). But jumping to that conclusion lands one on false etymology. Advice is a story in itself and hinges upon opinion . . . a belief that's usually offered free and worth every penny of that. So observed George Burns, when he remarked, "Too bad all the people who know how to run the country are busy driving cabs and cutting hair".

In the same vein William Safire, in the preface to his *Words of Wisdom,* offers this bit of advice. "The creeping commercialization of counsel has led to a sonic boom within the advice industry. If the advice explosion continues, we will become a nation of sheeplike advisees, hooked on direction by consultants, traumatized by the admonitions of moralizers, cowed by the expertise of specialists, bulldozed by the authority of pundits, inundated by the wave of detailed instructions pounded in by the vast how-to hierarchy." In a word, it's overload.

How did we first get advice? It invaded English from the French **advis,** Old French **a vis,** fathered by the phrase **ce m'est a vis,** which translates to my view is, or it seems to me. The phrase is a descendent of the Vulgar Latin **mi est visum,** visum the past participle of **videre,** to see.

Turning back to legitimate members of the turning clan, we find **tournament,** from the Old French **tourneier,** to tourney, earlier the Latin **tornare.** Medieval knights on horseback jousting and tilting one another made many a turn to avoid an

adversarial lance. Although a sport, a fall could prove injurious, requiring, you guessed it, a **tourniquet**, twisted to compress vessels and prevent the loss of blood. ⁊

† See "Behind Those Titles"

In Port

I T'S A HARBOR FOR docking your boat, an entrance to a courtyard for your car, a business yet a sport, a place wherein you may partake of dinner, especially with wine and beer. It's one of the basic nautical terms required of sailors, yet it describes a common labor as well as a female attorney.

It's a word of **opportunity**. It started as the I-E **per** and invaded our lexicon as **port**. Per expressed thoughts of leading, crossing or going through, as through a valley or mountain pass. When per-

went through the Mediterranean the Romans enlarged it to **portus,** a port or harbor that vessels passed into.

Thanks to the French we have that elegant term to describe a covered entrance to a courtyard that shelters us when entering or leaving our coach . . . a **port-cochere.**
And further underlying protection offered by ports is the **portcullis,** from the Middle French **porte** plus **coleice,** meaning flowing or sliding, and referring to those medieval grates that slid vertically to permit, or prevent, passage to many a castle.

Understandably, when crossing or going through, one may convey, hence the Greeks' **poreuein** or carry, and the Romans' **portare,** to carry something that we classify as **portable.** Not all carried necessarily is tangible. **Reporters** engage in **reportage,** carrying back newsworthy events.

Oporto (The **Port**) a coastal trading center in NW Portugal, well known as a **portal** for wine shipments, gave us the wine of the same name. Relatedly, **Portugal** was sired by the similar sounding **Portucale** of the Middle Ages, in turn from the Latin **Portus Cale**, the region behind the port of **Cale**.

Logically, shipping out of a port is to **export** and shipping in is to **import**. Contrary to contemporary wisdom that embraces a favorable balance of trade of exports over imports, the latter became the more **important**. The opposing frivolous is not "exportant", our language not tidy enough to give us such a word.

Whether exporting or importing, succeeding requires capitalizing upon **opportunities**. It's a benign wind that guides our ships toward port... from the Latin **opportunus**, the equivalent of **ob** (toward) plus **portus, a harbor.** A slack wind to port was an **inopportune** time to sail.

Why port as the left side of a ship (when facing the bow from the vantage of the stern)? The explanation is progressively speculative, but a tidy story. First we must accept that in sailing days of yore, oars on nascent sailing vessels were mounted on the right side of the boat, as was the rudder or **steerboard**, which became **starboard**. Why on the right? Possibly because we instinctively favored right over left, the collective "we" mostly being right-handed.[†]

To prevent damaging the oars or steerboard, boats were docked on their left or **larboard**, the latter bearing a long history. It hails from **laborde**, an alteration of the Middle English **laddeboarde**, from the Middle English **laden**, Old English **hladan**, both meaning to load on board, that is the side of a ship. Larboard is in agreement with its antithesis starboard, but the similar sound of lar- and star-, so goes the logic, was the cause of disagreement and confusion when orders were shouted from the bridge. Thus larboard logically gave way to port, the side docked to port.

Equally folksy is the derivation of **posh** for elegant, luxurious or stylish, and as an acronym for the phrase **port out, starboard home**.

This bit of linguistic legerdemain holds that the British once paid a premium for POSH-stamped steamship tickets if they desired to be berthed on the more comfortable or shady side of the ship. This translated to the port side, facing north for example on an eastern voyage out, and to the starboard side when returning home, to enjoy the same exposure.

That may be posh, but it doesn't wash, according to most etymologists. They look to Romany, the language of the Gypsies, for the clues to posh. The Romany half or posh, as in **posh-houri** (half pence) and **posh-kooroona** (half crown) evolved to the slang use of posh for money of any denomination, eventually to become descriptive of something swank or expensive.

Not so elegant is the pursuit of **porterage**. Nevertheless, our **porter,** a descendant of the French **porteur,** and the Latin **portare**, to carry, left us with a rich heritage of spin-offs. He could, for example, repair to the **porterhouse** and unwind from the day's burdens with a bottle of **porter**, a cheap but strong ale, first popularized in the early 1700s, and presumably appropriate for his budget. Later his choice of an entree was indeed choice . . . a **porterhouse steak**, a cut between the prime rib and the sirloin, and first popularized at a New York City porterhouse in the early 1800s.

As a real sport or bon vivant at the porterhouse our porter could appear somewhat **portly**, that is heavy or stout, a far, pejorative cry from the word's original sense that characterized one's bearing as stately or dignified. "So myche portlye pride, with pursys penyles", reflects a 14th-century sense of the word.

And why are we **sports**? Look to the archaic Middle English, Old French **desport,** which equated to games and amusements, in turn from the Middle Latin **disportare,** a carrying away (**dis**) from the serious business of work. Through the process of **aphesis** (the loss of an unstressed vowel or syllable, thanks to the Greek **aphienai,** to let go) we have shrunk the word to simply sport. All of this gets stood on its head with modern professional sports definitely qualifying as serious business.

In contrast to aphesis, we lengthen words by adding a syllable, a process named **prosthesis, pros** (to) plus **thesis**, from the Greek **tithenai** (put, set down). In addition to playing with words we set down many things via prosthesis . . . advancing propositions, composing essays, even adding dentures or body parts.

We also lengthen or compound words by smashing them together. Such were coined **portmanteau** words by Lewis Carroll in his *Through the Looking Glass*: "You see, it's like a portmanteau . . . there are two meanings packed into one." For example, **slithy** combines **lithe** and **slimy**, as he explained to Alice. Packing isappropriate, as the French portmanteau is a double-sided trunk for carrying several cloaks. Portmanteau itself is compounded from carry plus the French **manteau**, a sleeveless cape or cloak that envelopes and covers, as does a **mantle**. And so we have **motels** (motorist plus hotel) and **smog** (smoke plus fog) plus numerous other telescopings.

Port survives in eponymy. The I-Es gave us a leading sense to port, and in lockstep, the Romans followed with the female name **Portia**, denoting one who could lead to safety.

Appropriately the witty and charming heiress of Shakespeare's *Merchant of Venice* was a Portia. Disguised as a lawyer, she successfully defended her lover's friend, Antonio, from being excised of a pound of flesh, the penalty for defaulting on a debt to the spiteful money-lender, Shylock.

Splitting hairs, Portia eschews a generous monetary settlement, demanding instead Shylock take exactly a pound of flesh, not a hair's worth more or less, not a jot of blood, a challenge impossible for Shylock. Thanks to this famed comedy, Portia can refer to a female attorney.

It's unclear if Portia carried a **portfolio**, as do most in her profession. Contrastingly a minister without portfolio doesn't represent a specific governmental department and therefore literally doesn't carry a briefcase. Portfolio is compacted from the

Latin portare (to carry) plus **foglio**, (a sheet) from the Latin **folium**, a leaf. Thus we have the Italian **portafoglio**, later our portfolio, a briefcase for carrying papers. . .and with some license here, a portfolio of ports. ✌

† See "Righteous Predomination"

Adaptable

C LAY IS PLIABLE, COPPER ductile, gold malleable, rubber elastic, a hazel wand lithesome (as Tennyson reminded us) and uranium transmutable (into energy). But, in the kaleidoscope of worldly change animals display **adaptability**, from the Latin adaptare (**ad-**, to, plus **aptare**, join) meaning adjust.

"We see beautiful adaptation everywhere and in every part of the organic world," observed Darwin, referring to the biological sense of an organism becoming altered by natural selection, thus enabling it to survive in a changing environment. Perhaps flashing through Darwin's consciousness were images of tortoises and finches from his days in the Galapagos Islands.

Although tortoises (known as **galapagos** in Spanish) through-out the islands were almost identical in appearance, on an island abundant in grass their necks were quite short. Yet on another island where the only edible food was shrub-high, their necks were quite long. Similarly, many species of finches there developed specialized beaks. The cactus finch, for example, uses his elongat-ed bill for extracting pulp from prickly fruit. The large ground finch has an exceptionally strong bill for cracking hard-shelled nuts. And the small-billed ground finch has no trouble delicately pick-ing insects off the backs of tortoises and iguanas.

Man certainly is adaptive. Joked Bernard Shaw, "The reason-able man adapts himself to the world: The unreasonable one persists in trying to adapt the world to himself. Therefore all progress depends upon the unreasonable man."

Regardless, man would be hard put not to bow to the breadth of another creature's adaptability . . . that of the whale. He's been at it for some 50 million years!

Its historical adaptation is fascinating, if not mind-boggling. Fossil evidence proves that the whale's ancestor, some 50 million years ago, was a four-legged carnivore. It gradually entered inshore waters to catch fish and developed a taste for morsels of the sea.

Evolution then took a lengthy but natural course. To facili-tate swimming, webbing developed between the whale's toes, and its body became streamlined to reduce drag. (Perhaps if we and our progeny started a 30-million-year swim we would become streamlined!)

A look at a whale embryo reveals a tail, hind-limb buds, nostrils at the front of its head, fingers on its hands, and external ear lobes, all disappearing as the embryo grows, its gestation thus mimicking eons of the species development.

When born the tail emerges as flukes, nostrils have receded from snout to top of head, forelegs have become flippers, and since the whale now hears through water instead of air, external ears have been replaced with an internal hearing mechanism. However, some vestiges of its land-roaming days remain . . . chambered stomachs, for ruminating like a cow, hip bones and hind-limb buds and outside ear cartilage.

By no means has the whale grown tired of adapting. Consider the gray. Within months after birth in Baja California breeding waters, gray calves begin a 5,000-mile journey northward from tepid Mexican waters to frigid Arctic seas, a record-long migration for mammals.

Blue behemoths, up to 25 feet long at birth double their weight in their first week, then settle down to a mere 200 pound gain daily. Approximately seven months later upon weaning they have grown to 50 feet in length and weigh around 23 tons . . . thanks to mother's milk, a heavy cream four times richer than the milk we drink.

A sperm whale is comfortable at sea level or 3,500 feet below. He can spend up to an hour and a half there looking for giant squid, his favorite meal, then quickly return to the surface for a breath . . . all this without concern for the extreme pressure crushing its lungs or inducing bends.

Inclement weather? No problem for southern right whales. They have been observed using their flukes as a sail. Setting the flukes to the proper angle propels them at high speed with a minimal expenditure of energy.

That these mighty, marvelous, marine mammals chose to return to our common biological breeding waters gives us something to ponder. ⫯

Extended Terms of Business

DESPITE IRS THREATS TO glance askance at so-called
martini-driven lunches, breaking bread with business **companions** is a time-honored tradition, literally for the same reason
we have **company** over the weekend. The **com** of company and
companions equates to **cum** plus **panis**, that is bread, all of which
comes from the **pantry**. Speculation holds that panis derived from
the Latin **pascere**, in turn the I-E **pa**, to nourish . . . as does the
sales representative hope to nourish relationships with his pros-
pects over lunch.

Companies take many different forms. Take the broker. His
history is awash in booze. In Anglo-French, he was an **abrocour**,
wine merchant, a sense he picked up from the Spanish and their
alboroque, a gift, especially a drink taken to seal a transaction.
The gift idea is also reflected in the Arabic **al-buruk**, meaning gift
or gratuity. But the Old French started us down this path with
their **brokiere**, one who broaches a wine cask. (Now we have
extended the sense to opening a subject by broaching it.) The
brokiere eventually became a wine salesman, and in 14th-century
England expanded his talents to more risky enterprises, becoming
a pimp, pander and later a marriage broker.

When engaged in risky enterprises a business may be termed
speculative, its opportunities hinging upon guess and conjecture.
Such a company literally views its market from afar, so discloses
the Latin **specular**, meaning to watch over, explore. It's a derivative of **specula**, a watch tower, in turn from **specere**, to look, in
this case somewhat anxiously.

As an **employee** of a company, one may feel locked in. And for
good reason. Implied in the 13th century **emplien** was the sense of
being devoted, later applied to one who works for hire. All this

evolved from the Latin **implicare**, to infold. Logically followed the concept of the **incentive**, wherein company policy embraced measures to **incite** those folded in to more enthusiastic and productive efforts.

Strange as it may seem, this has much to do with music. For incentive ultimately flows from the Latin **incinere**, to play a musical instrument, as does the related **canere** mean to sing. The Romans apparently subscribed to 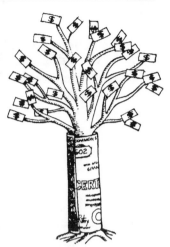 the idea that music could be provocative, arousing. No doubt that an employee who whistles while he works is highly motivated. Historically, we have confounded incentive with the Latin **incensive**, a derivative of **incendere**, to set a fire . . . something a sales manager strives to do under his sales force.

Of course a major objective of business is to lock in **customers**. Hopefully, they are **accustomed** to dealing with your firm. Custom and **costume**, the latter a style of dress worn for a special event or calling, are doublets that flow from the Latin **consuere**, meaning to make one's own. In a similar vein a customary practice, or a garb worn by a monk or a nun, is a **habit**, as is the kelp forest **habitat** the natural environment of the sea otter. They all **have** it, thanks to the Latin **habere**.

Cash customers are gradually becoming a custom of the past in this day of expanded credit[†] and use of plastic. Cash is actually named for the box where money was stored, the Old French **casse** and Latin **cassa**, both boxes. The spot where a proprietor chose to hide his casse when closing up shop is the **cache**, not related to cash, but instead is from the Old French **cacher**, to hide ... a duty of the **cashier**, who owes his designation to the Middle French **caissier**, a treasurer responsible for the money box.

Similarly **money** is not named after a synonym having any-thing to do with a medium of exchange, but instead from a mint. In Roman mythology one of the titles of the goddess Juno was **Moneta**. Some etymologists believe Moneta was inspired by the Greek goddess of memory, **Mnemosune**, and derived from the Latin **monere**, to remind, warn, which reminds us of precious little about money. What we do know is that money was coined in a temple honoring Juno Moneta. Thus moneta became known as the **mint**, where coins were struck, and in Old French **moneie**, the actual coins.

When **charging** a purchase a customer is literally loading himself with debt. Charging flows from the Latin **carricare**, to load a **carrus**, a wagon*, a task we continue with our shopping carts some 2,000 years later. The synonymous use of charging/loading is not confined to debt. We once loaded or charged muskets with powder and shot and either unloaded the gun or discharged it, **dis-** giving the opposite sense to carricare.

Back to the debt. If not settled, the debtor could be charged with a crime. This also brings to mind the possibility of **garnishing** the perpetrator's salary, which has absolutely nothing to do with the radish florets and parsley sprigs that may accompany a shrimp salad. Right? Wrong! The logic is thin, but goes something like this: The court-ordered garnish stems from the Old French **garnir**, meaning to fortify, to warn, and later to equip with elaborate and more decorative armor, thus shifting to a sense of adornment, whether mounted on a tower or appearing on a plate.

Now, if we want to limit liability (to actual amounts invested) and facilitate transfers of ownership (through stock) we can **incorporate**. The concept is based upon the Latin **corpus**, a body, in this case an inanimate one that lives on regardless whether shareholders do so or not.

Despite the rather recent (15th century) use of **stock** to designate corporate ownership, its etymology is fuzzy. The Old

English **stocc** was a tree trunk. Its meaning in the 13th century expanded into a sense of supply, not a bad idea especially at the onset of winter. The supply connotation gradually shifted into money, then capital, which was divisible into shares by the 15th century. The latter sense probably evolved because money is the essence of a company, enabling it to grow, as did the stocc, and hopefully one's shares in a corporation. The possible **dividends** therefrom are more straightforward, a product of the Latin **dividere**, to **divide**, in this case profits.

If the company obtains funds from the **bond** market, it's **bound** to repay principal and interest. In fact it's in the vital **interest** of the company to pay bond obligations when due. The Latin **esse**, meaning is, to be, contains the vital sense. **Inter** conveys that this vital matter is between two entities, bondholder and issuer, or perhaps represents the idea that payment is for use of principal between two interest payment dates.

Our Germanic **bind** goes back to the I-E **bhendh**, like the bands which tightly hold a bundle of sticks in place and the Sanskrit **badhnati**, their binds. It's also a relative of the Hindi **bandhnu**, a method of tie-dying cloth to produce a variegated coloration, as in our **bandana**.

Tied-up and choking in debt a corporation is forced to end its free spending ways and **economize**, just as one would at home by managing resources more prudently. Just ask the Greeks. We inherited their concept of economizing from their **oikos**, house, plus **nemein**, manage.

If economizing and restructuring fails, perhaps there's enough value in the company to interest a **merger** partner. This could involve intense **negotiations**, a process fraught with stress and strain. At least that's what the Romans thought. Our predecessor for negotiations is their **negotium: neg**, not, plus **otium**, (of) ease or leisure.

The **merger** concept comes from the Latin **mergere**, to dive or become **immersed** in a liquid. It's akin to the Sanskrit **majjati**, he dives, bathes, and is based upon the I-E root **mezg**, to plunge into water. How appropriate that **emerge** so often seems to be the business writer's verb of choice to characterize a company leaving the protection of a bankruptcy chapter, no longer **submerged** in a sea of red ink is the **firm.**

It's with solid rationale that a business entity is termed a firm. Like the company that successfully emerged from bankruptcy, firm denotes an entity solid, not yielding, reliable. More basic, the Latin **firmare**, to affix, **affirm**, was picked up by the Spanish as **firma**, their signature, used as the legal name of the firm. More recently in America it is exemplified by the John Hancock Insurance Company's logo in the form of the boldest signature to appear beneath the Declaration of Independence.

The history of a firm is also grounded down on the **farm**. The Latin firmare, evolved to the Latin **firma**, the rent a tenant paid a **farmer**. Not until the 1660s was the sense of farming transferred from handling money to getting one's hands into the soil.

Perhaps the value perceived in the merged company focuses on its **patents**. Patents, from the Old French **lettre patente**, meaning open letter, ironically is a device used to close competition. The Latin **patentem**, or lying open, from **patere**, to open, reflects that patents were originally written on flat sheets of parchment, not rolled in volumes[‡] and therefore are clear, evident, for all to see. Why the phrase patent leather? This term of quality prevailed after the original patents were granted for the process of making leather hard, glossy and smooth.

Of course a business relies on government for more than patent protection. It seeks shelter under the foliage of governmental arbors, as did a young Samuel Morse buttonhole congressmen under a shady elm tree in front of Washington's Willard Hotel in support of his newly invented telegraph. This shelter, from the old High German **lauba** and Latin **lobia**, was adopted by the English as a covered walk, anteroom, or **lobby**, later adopted by American **lobbyists** for pitching their causes. ‹›

†*See* From the Heart
*See Getting Around
‡ *See* Taking Liberties

Some Call It Work

S TRANGE AS IT MAY SEEM, music of the church, vital body parts, a company and perhaps its propaganda, main street and, yes, even sex are all related. The etymological glue that holds all this together is the Greek **organon**, allied to **ergon** in turn a derivative of the I-E **werg**, the latter two terms meaning **work**.

Historians credit the Greeks with inventing the organ around the third century BC. It originally was named a **hydraulus (hydro,** water, plus **aulos,** pipe) because an integral tub of water helped regulate required air pressure. Soon it became known as the organon simply because this marvelous instrument worked, thanks to energy created under air pressure in its bellows.

Etymologically it's an easy leap to a biological **organ** or a group of tissues, such as the heart of an animal or stamen of a flower, that work on a specialized task. In turn groups of mutually interdependent organs function as an **organism**, as in a plant or an animal.

Work requires **energy**, understandably produced from werg via the Greek **energeia, energos** and the Late Latin **energia**. Traces of werg are also present when working with metal, as in **metallurgy** (the Greek **metallon,** meaning mine). We also acknowledge the manual work entailed in **surgery**, once referred to in Middle English as **surgerie**, from the Old French **cirurgerie**, in turn the Greek **kheirourgia**, that is **ourgia**, work by **kheir**, hand.

Shipwrights, millwrights and playwrights all acknowledge the efforts of their labors. **Wright**, a skilled worker, is a product of the Old English **wryhta**, a relative of the Old English **wrohte**, which gave us our participle **wrought**, an almost archaic way of saying something is finely or elaborately worked.

In the 13th century we adopted another term that inconspicuously implies loads of work, the **bulwark**. It descended from the Middle Low German **bolwerk** . . . **bolle**, from the Old Norse **bolr**, that is tree or the plank that it yields, plus **werk**. It apparently required lots of werk (werg) to make a fort or a rampart from a bolle, and you certainly hoped that it worked.

This leads us right into **boulevard**, a French twist on bulwark, possibly because this broad thoroughfare was lined with trees, but more likely because it was usually constructed upon the site of a razed rampart.

The I-E believed in work, as evidenced by another verb to describe his labors, **op:** to work and produce abundantly. Op brings us back to surgery, an **operation**, but also leads us to more pleasant experiences, as when listening to an **opus**, a musical work, or an **opera**, a dramatic musical work, which requires the **cooperation** of various musicians. And for a real arty word to describe an artist's entire work, we stole from the French their **oeuvre** from the Latin opus and related to the Sanskrit **apas**, both meaning a work.

As an organ works, so does an **organization**, its employees motivated by management in any number of communications devices, including the company **house organ**. Individuals feeling unsettled long to get **organized**. The process isn't always obvious, per Paul Valery's observation that "politeness is organized indifference."

Sex, regarded as pleasurable, is hardly equated with work, though sex involves organs engaged in intense activity. Boiling in fervor and lust, the ensuing **orgasm** has at its root the I-E **uerg**, to swell. However, if we raise the number of players to an **orgy** level that involves feasting, drinking, dancing and mass copulation, work it is. The Greeks and their cult of Dionysus engaged in these fertility rituals known as their **orgia**, from their ergon, formerly the I-E **werg** . . . both words of work.

Almost any unrestrained activity or overpowering scene can be depicted in orgasmic terms. A field of vibrantly blooming wildflowers may be described as an orgy of bursting colors; so, too, a van Gogh work.

Organismic entities abound in almost infinite varieties, none so complex or sophisticated as man. In the words of Charles Darwin, ". . . man with all his noble qualities . . . with his god-like intellect . . . with all his exalted powers . . . still bears in his bodily frame the indelible stamp of his lowly origin. He (has) risen, though not through his own exertions, to the very summit of the **organic** scale."

In his quest to explain the origin of the species the industrious Darwin certainly wasn't **allergic** to work. Even when we are laid low from an allergy work continues, strange work that is, from the Greek **allos**, different, plus **ergon**, work.

Further substantiating the strange nature of work is the observation of Burton Rascoe (writer, anthologist) that, "What no spouse of a writer can ever understand is that the writer is working when staring out the window." 🕭

Ships of State

THOSE WHO GOVERN often allude to steering their ships of
state†, an etymologically correct choice of metaphors, as
the Greek **kybernan** and later the Latin **gubernare**, both meaning to steer a ship, with a sense of control and holding in check,
evolved to our similar sounding verb **govern**.

To the numerous Greek and Roman terms
of government steered our way we have tacked
on many suffixal **isms**. So many that in this
day of isms the word has justifiably earned the
status of a stand-alone noun, indicating a doctrine or system of government.

One of the more fascinating isms is **fascism**.
It sprang from **Fasci 'd Combattimento**, an
organization spearheaded by Benito Mussolini to rally unemployed
and disheartened WWI veterans into a political force. The organization's icon was the **fascis**, a bundle of sticks with an ax projecting from one end, a throwback capitalizing on Roman heritage.

Roman magistrates carried **fasces** as symbols of power, lowered
in respectful salute, but always on prominent display with its sticks
representing the threat of the whip, and the ax ever remindful of
the finality of execution. The fascis developed into the Late Latin
and French **fascina**, and in the 1600s into a **fascine**, a longer
bundle of sticks used in building earthworks and in strengthening
ramparts.

The resurrection of the Roman fascis was not exclusively Mussolini's idea. Prior to WWI the United States marked one side of
its dime with a fascis, an updated representation of the "Don't tread
on me" slogan, as a warning of its power to any potential enemies
of liberty. By 1945 the mint got off the dime and removed the icon

shared with Mussolini by replacing it with a more palatable symbol, the torch of liberty.

By blaming foreigners for Italy's post WWI plight Mussolini was able to hold his misguided followers spellbound, that is **fascinated,** a word that once meant to bewitch, later to charm or captivate. The Latin **fascinare**, to bewitch, is the foundation of fascinate, and is a derivative of **fascinum**, which to the Romans meant, logically enough, an evil eye but incredibly also a penis, thanks to **Fascinus**, a Latin god of sorcery. Apparently the phallic symbol was often worn around the neck to serve as an amulet, a reverse spellbinder, to ward off the evil eye.

Also sowed from seeds of WWI discontent, and related onerous reparations demanded of Germany at the treaty of Versailles, was Hitler's **Nazism**. Nazism was fascism in its ugliest form but shares no verbal lineage. It's simply short for the Nationalsozialistische Deutsche Arbeiter-Partei (National Socialist Worker's Party), a mouthful which indeed required scrunching. Small wonder Mark Twain's observation: Whenever the literary German dives into a sentence, that is the last you are going to see of him 'til he emerges on the other side of his Atlantic with his verb in his mouth.

Communism deserves a short shrift. Tried at various times since Plato's Republic, the modern sense of the word stems from the Latin **communis**, a sharing of commonalties, from **munia**, equating to a number of things. . .mainly offices, duties, gifts and presents plus the **com** form of together. The munia sounded and was too good to be true. The only thing shared are duties and the gifts are hardly worth sharing. The Soviets should have been forewarned. Ideas from anyone advocating Platonic love, that is love free from sensual desire between members of the opposite sex living together, are highly suspect.

For a heady ism we have **capitalism**, generally regarded as a system wherein industry is owned and operated by individuals and corporations as opposed to the state. It's derived from the Latin

capitalis, caput, or head*. The suffixal **al,** meaning related to, plus the doctrinal ism, gives capitalism the distinction of a double suffix, perhaps appropriate, as conservative **capitalists** leave nothing to chance.

Apparently we were comfortable relating our surroundings to body parts and in the process going head over heels with a very principal part, the caput or head. It eventually ended up being a **capital,** or head city; the captain who heads a ship or army contingent; and uppercase or capital letters at the beginning of a sentence. It invaded financial lexicon to denote wealth, as in capital or principal assets, essential for the good capitalistic life.

When capital applies to punishment, life is lost, the criminal becoming **decapitated.** Many a capitalist lost his head but managed to live, for example, Michael Milken, tripped up capitalizing on investor greed by illegally floating junk bonds.

Architecturally, a capital is the head city, or seat, of a government. The **capitol,** however, houses the U.S. Congress or a state legislature. The distinction is that the building mimics the temple of Jupiter at the head of Saturnian hill in Rome, named **Capitoline,** again from the ubiquitous caput.

From the same root but traveling a different route is capital's doublet **cattle,** also of capitalistic linkage. Spelled **catel** in Anglo and Old North French, formerly the Latin **capitalis,** it also pertains to the head. Therefore at one time, head of cattle was redundant. Catel, once movable property, became more restrictive in sense and eventually applied only to cattle, a recognized medium of exchange before the advent of money.‡

An ism espoused by most sovereignties as well as labor movements is **unionism.** Though it's hard to imagine a nation holding the **onion** as its symbol, the thought is not completely ludicrous. The Latin **unus,** one, became the Late Latin **unionem,** meaning an onion or a pearl. All this was logical to the Romans because the onion's many connected layers and the pearl's concentric crystalline layers, constructed of secretions from the oyster's or muscle's mantle tissue, each add up to interconnected entities.

The Latin unionem flowed to French as **oignon**, thence English in a bewildering series starting with **ungeon**, followed by **oinoin, unyon, onyon** and finally settling down as onion. In contrast unionem also invaded French as **union** then to English by first barely tripping over **unioun** before discarding its final "u."

And that's why we have union suits, or one-piece underwear. One bit of folk etymology claimed that the union suit originated during the Civil War, a product of the Union Army. It's even been embellished to the point that Grant wore his union suit to humiliate Lee in full dress at the Appomattox surrender. Etymologists yelled foul. The Union Army issue was a two-piece garment.

Also deeply immersed in our lexical heritage are some of the devices various isms employ to govern. Consider **parliament**. Its embryo was formed in the Greek **paraballein**, meaning to throw beside, that is compare, based upon **para**, beside, plus **bole**, to throw. The Late Latin **parabolare** gave us our parables, allegorical stories often relying on comparisons or analogies. This all leads to the French **parler**, to speak, and later their **parlour**, a place to speak. Hence the **parle** is a preoccupation of any parliament.

Many find **diets** hard to swallow, whether prescribed by a physician or run by a national assembly. Many etymologists claim that the two diets are not related. Yet offering a prime example that words, like cells, divide and multiply, a case can be made for a common parentage.

A national assembly or law-making **diet** owes its existence to the Greek **diaita**, meaning a course of life, which eventually became the Latin **diaeta**, **dieta**, a reference to ordinary daily duties, especially when it came to running the Holy Roman Empire. However, a possible link between the nourishing and governing diets lies in the flow of this same Greek diaita, a prescribed way of life, to the Old French **dieta**, which became the diet the doctor ordered.

Some further argue that day, from the I-E **diew**, the shining sky, which is observable only in the day time, later to become the Latin **dies**, or day, is somehow hidden in all this through its sense of daily routines. (So is **dial**, from the Latin dies, an instrument that relates the time from its shawdowy relationship with the sun.) The Germans certainly are cognizant of running their government on a daily basis. Their parliament, the **Reichtag** controls the affairs of the **Reich** (nation) every **Tag** (day).

Dissenters from the Greek connection can take nourishment by taking diaita back further. It's from the Greek **diaitasthai**, to lead one's life, in turn, it's speculated from **diaitan**, to separate food and drink, possibly a form of **diainysthai** . . . **dia**, apart, plus **ainysthai**, to take. But, like many diets, this explanation should be taken with a grain of salt.

And for an organization more out of step than in, we have the US **Congress**, which according to Latin definition is supposed to be composed of members who step, **gradi**, together, **con**. By implication they should take one step at a time, just as we took one **grade** at a time in school. Congress, however, has ample excuse for its continual **digressiveness**, wherein politics prevailing, it literally steps away from problems. In the 13th century a **congresse** came together to fight. Sounds like old times in today's Congress, and for that it deserves bad grades.

In agreement with us was the Supreme **Soviet**, that former body prone to collective head scratching after the launching of perestroika and glasnost and the ensuing disagreement among its rulers and republics. It, too, belied its founding concepts: **Suvetu** in Old Russian most clearly embraces agreement . . . **vetu**, meaning council, agreement, plus **su**, together.

Isms need their **archs**, the latter prevalent in all Germanic languages, including the Latin **archi**, and the Greek varieties of **arche**,

archi, and archos, for ruler. Relatedly our arch is a curved structure, as in the arc of a circle, and possibly stems from a Latin
version, the arcus, a bow and descendent of the I-E arku, a bow
and/or arrow. All this suggests that the modern combining form
-arch, denoting a leader or ruler, may have a tenuous link to rulers
who achieved status and power at least partially through their proficiency at archery, as did the legendary Robin Hood.

When it comes to leading, the Greeks always had a word for it.
The oligarch, from their oligarches, one of a few who rules, is
distinct by its olig, from oligos, meaning little or few. If the squab-
bling among the few is bothersome, you could move to a
monarchy, where the monarch is the sole ruler, thanks to
monarches, based upon monos, alone.

Our Grecian friends also came up with kratia, kratos for ruler,
which came down to us through the Late Latin cratia and Middle
French cracie, giving English a handy combining form -crat. Thus
we have the plutocrat, whose sole claim to power is wealth, from
the Greek plouto(s), wealth. And for absolute power there's the
autocrat, this authoritarian so designated by the prefix auto or
self. And for real snobs and egoists we have the aristocrats. They
are superior, the best rulers, this claim is based upon the Greek
aristos, once descriptive of the upper class, previously the warrior
class. There's a sense of strength underlying these rulers. The Greek
kratos also means strength and is possibly related to krays, something strong, or hard, which says something about many a ruler.

This brings us to the hard-headed anarchist, who believes in
an (not), that is no rule, and seeks to violently overthrow existing
governments without any plans for a successor regime.

For a less precipitous approach to bringing down the government, trust a bureaucracy ˙˙ or hierarchy, the latter inherited from
the ecclesiastical world. Originally it meant the power of the priest,
from hiero, Greek for holy or sacred. In the modern secular world
it denotes a system of layers of government with servants ranked

one above the other and often rankling one another. Eventually the ponderous layers grow massive, become ensnared in their own fossilization . . . the "gubernare" of many a ship of state rendered rudderless. ✒

† See "Circum Stantia"
* See "Behind Those Titles"
‡ See "Terms Of Business"
** See "Big Wheels"

Culinary Concoctions: Eponyms III

WE ANTICIPATE THE AROMA of exotic spices and succulent flavors with our cuisine. But also served up is a smorgasbord of "eponymistic" food-for-thought . . . whether partaking in an **epicurean** delight at the fashionable **Ritz** or simply grabbing a **hamburger** on the run from a fast-food outlet.

The roots of epicure run deep. Epikourous, a Greek philosopher (342-270 BC) saw nothing wrong with pleasurable pursuits and so advocated them "to be the beginning and end of a blessed life," and presumably appropriate at any time between those two eventful extremes. His was not an open-ended invitation to a licentious lifestyle, but couched within boundaries of propriety and virtue.

Later generations, however, focused on the pleasure angle, especially sensual, possibly and falsely stealing a page from the book of Epicurus, as the Romans spelled it, because his school welcomed the participation of women, not a practice condoned by many other Greek philosophers. The sensual angle gradually shifted to a sense of food and drink, something one with a sensitive taste, like a contemporary epicurean, most appreciates, as Sydney Smith so versified: "Serenely full, the epicure would say, /Fate cannot harm me, I have dined today."

And when dining, why not have a drink, which brings up the thought that we toast the health of others at the peril of our own. **Scotch** as an eponym speaks for itself. One Scotsman, however, was most vociferous in his veneration of the malted barley: If a body could just find oot the exac' proper proportion and quantity that ought to be drunk every day, and keep to that, I verily vow that he might leeve forever, without dying at a', and that doctors and kirkyards (churchyards) would go oot of fashion.

Bourbon, the corn-based whiskey was originally produced in the US in Bourbon County, Kentucky, in turn named after France's Bourbon kings, who prevailed during a 200 year dynasty and were the first to distill it.

Contemplating the ancestry of a **bloody Mary**, is enough to make one gag on this vodka-tomato juice concoction. It owes its name to Mary I, Mary of Tudor (1516-58), the illegitimate daughter of King Henry VIII and the queen of England and Ireland. Though she reigned for only five years, Mary I managed to put to death more than 300 of her subjects, including a former queen, Lady Jane Grey (and her husband) and the Archbishop of Canterbury, Thomas Cranmer, but also imprisoned or persecuted many others for simply being politically incorrect in their support of Protestantism . . . a thought that could easily drive one to drink.

Whatever your choice, it's all **booze**, which has a disputed ancestry. Folk etymology cites Colonel **Booze,** a Philadelphia (some say Kentucky) distiller, who bottled his liquor in the 1840s in bottles shaped in the image of log cabins.

But booze may have an older heritage. The Middle English verb **bousen** meant to drink deeply. Bousen is related to the Middle Dutch **busen,** that is to rebel or carouse, a trait of the "over-boozed."

That's a condition definitely to be eschewed when **Puttin' on the Ritz,** as Irving Berlin would put it.

For a **ritzy** style, we owe thanks to Cesar **Ritz** (1850-1918) a Swiss who founded the Ritz Hotel chain, famed as a symbol of ultimate luxury and splendor. Noel Coward, while dining there, couldn't help noticing Woolworth heiress Barbara Hutton flashing her meticulously manicured fingernails while she dined at a nearby table. The verbose Coward also couldn't help himself from lyrically describing the scene:

> *Children of the Ritz*
> *Sleek and civilized*
> *Frightfully surprised*
> *We know just how we want our quails done*
> *And then we go and have our nails done.*

However your choice of an entree at the Ritz may be a **Châteaubriand** steak. It's all because of Vicomte Francois Rene de Châteaubriand (1768-1848) a French writer and statesman. His favorite steak was a thick slice of tenderloin[†], often served with a **Béarnaise** sauce, a blend of egg yolks, shallots, tarragon, butter, vinegar and perhaps white wine and chervil, an eponym of the District of **Béarn** in SW France, its legendary origin.

And no dinner is worth its "eponymistic" salt without a **Caesar salad,** not named for the famed Roman Emperor, who probably holds a record for honorific eponyms[*], but for the lesser known Caesar Gardini, owner-operator of the restaurant Caesar's Palace in Tijuana, Mexico. Once when low on provisions but high on customers who dropped in en route home from Baja, California Jai Alai games and bull fights, Gardini innovatively contrived a salad from a few ingredients off the shelf: lightly tossed romaine lettuce, garlic-flavored croutons, olive oil, lemon juice, grated parmesan cheese, egg and **Worcestershire** sauce (a product of Worcestershire, the county, that is **shire,** seat of **Worcester**

County, England). Romanoff's in Hollywood later popularized the salad and is credited for enhancing it with a touch of anchovy.

And for fashionable tableware we have **Wedgwood**, developed by Josiah Wedgwood (1730-95). He built his pottery works near Hanley, England, as well as a village there for his employees and named it **Etruria**, as Wedgwood's designs were inspired by ancient Etruscan ware made in Etruria, Italy.

Definitely not appropriately served on Wedgwood at the Ritz is the **sandwich**, unless of course you are being served the finger variety at high tea. We do put the finger on an Englishman, however, for originating the sandwich. John Montagu, the fourth Earl of Sandwich (1718-92) and a habitual gambler, was loathe to leave the gaming table, even for a meal. One such time, at a 24-hour session, he ordered a slice of meat between two slices of bread, and thus was born the sandwich. (As First Lord of the Admiralty, Montagu was honored by Captain James Cook, who named a group of islands Cook discovered in the Pacific as the Sandwich Islands. Today we know them as the Hawaiian Islands.)

Perhaps our most popular sandwich is the **hamburger**, an eponym that explains why hamburger contains no ham. The original term for this morsel was **Hamburg** steak, or ground beef, which originated in Germany's Hamburg, that is home (**Ham**) plus fort, fortress (**burg**). German immigrants brought the idea to the United States, where it was Americanized in the form of a sandwich.

Like many recipes, development of the hamburger was more evolutionary than revolutionary, and some credit, at least for its nascent form, belongs to the Russian **Tartars**. Tartars, from the Latin **tartarus**, the Greek **tartaros**, meaning hell, raised just that under Genghis Khan (1162-1227) throughout Asia and Eastern Europe. They were as tough as their meat obtained from poor quality Asian cattle. To make their raw meat more digestible the Tartars shredded it, an idea they introduced to the Germans, who enhanced it Hamburg style with local spices, including onion and garlic, and eventually cooked it. The raw version, however, survives as a gourmet dish with capers and raw egg with a French twist, called steak **tartare**.

And for the ubiquitous **frankfurter** we must credit another German city, **Frankfurt am Main.** In the mid-1800s the butcher's guild of Frankfurt devised a spiced and smoked sausage that was stuffed into a thin casing. Its curved shape, so legend goes, mimicked that of a butcher's beloved dachshund. The Frankfurter thus earned the sobriquet **dachshund sausage**, perhaps encouraging its later Americanization as a **hot dog** soon after the turn of the century.

Americans also stole **wiener** and **wienie** from the German **Wienerwurst. Wurst** is German for sausage, specially made to satisfy the palates of one in **Wein,** German for the Austrian city of **Vienna.** Sausage in Old French was **saussiche,** from the Latin **salsus,** that is **salted‡** as is our sausage.

The butchers of Frankfurt cannot take total credit for the frankfurter. Evolution here goes back much further than that of the hamburger. Approximately 3,500 years ago Babylonians stuffed animal intestines with their versions of spices and meats.

Despite its condemnation by the Catholic Church and several Roman Emperors the sausage survived. Its ritualistic association with the yearly orgiastic Lupercalian festival (named after the pagan god Lupercus) brought down the wrath of church and government to ban both the festival and the sausage. In addition to sexual initiation rites the festival encouraged the practice of boys drawing names of girls from name boxes, thus establishing partners for the Lupercalian year. More bizarre was the custom of boys, clad only in goat skins around their loins, running amok and striking women with goat skins, a custom purported to make their victims more fertile or to lessen labor pains for those already pregnant.

Eventually Saint Valentine's Day, sponsored by the church, christianized Lupercalia and encouraged participants instead to emulate the lives of saints. The advent of postal service provided a means of getting around the randomness of the name box and helped popularize Valentines. Through it all bootlegged sausage, though a sin, remained popular, and as with fish on Friday, its ban eventually was rescinded.

If you are in a dessert mood there's always **peach Melba,** peaches with ice cream. Several versions of the origin of peach Melba exist. All, however, involve Dame Nellie Melba (1861-1931), the Australian operatic soprano.

So one story goes, the famed French chef, Auguste Escoffier, created peach Melba and served it in high ambiance within a swan of ice to Dame Melba at the Ritz Carlton in London in honor of her performance of Lohengrin at Covent Garden. (Of Scottish and Spanish descent, Melba's real name was Helen Porter Mitchell, and her married name Armstrong, but she assumed the stage name Melba after her native city of **Melbourne,** in turn named after a British prime minister.)

Apparently Dame Melba cut quite a culinary swath. **Melba-toast,** crisp, dry, thin slices of toast, and **Melba sauce,** a clear raspberry dessert topping, are also named in her honor.

Though we have barely scraped the bottom of our "eponymistic" plate, it's time we push away from the table. But first we must have a cup of **coffee.** The drink's name we borrowed from the Turkish **kahveh,** in turn from the Arabic **qahwah,** inspired from **Kaffa,** Abyssinia (present-day Ethiopia) and home of the shrub **Coffea arabica.**

In the seventh century a goatherd, named Kaldi, noticed his flock appeared what we, in present-day parlance, would term wired. Noticing their penchant for nibbling coffee berries, he tried some and confirmed his suspicions. It wasn't long before he and fellow Arabs were drying and infusing the berries into qahwah. The Turks soon picked up the idea as their kahveh, France its **cafe,** and English in several forms from **chaoua** to eventually coffee. It would be difficult not to get across understandably your desire for a cup of the stuff anywhere. Coffee, like brother, mother or father, is recognizable in any form . . . Portuguese cafe, Italian **caffe**, German **Kaffee**, Danish-Norwegian-Swedish **kaffe**, Dutch **koffie**, and even Russian **kofe**.

If all this drives you to a stronger drink, we can return to Caesar (100-44 BC). Your after-dinner **sherry**, hails from the Spanish **vino de Xeres**, also known as **Urbs Caesaris**, the city of Caesar. And for a time-honored drink, there is always **Benedictine**, first produced in the early 1500s by monks who named their liqueur in honor of St. Benedict, circa 500.**

Drinking too much after dinner, though, according to one tale, raises the specter of an unsaintly Benedict named Samuel. This reputed roue of New York's society set supposedly greeted many a morning with a heavy hangover. On such occasions he often ordered a breakfast of poached eggs with bacon on toast, all topped with **hollandaise** sauce (undoubtedly unaware he was popularizing an eponym contrived by the Dutch). A chef at the Waldorf, according to this version, fine-tuned the dish by substituting ham and an English muffin and named it **eggs Benedict** after his patron.

If Benedict would have ordered a **croissant** for breakfast, his choice of this buttery, flaky roll would symbolize a celebration of a military campaign of the 17th century. The croissant, French for **crescent**, was invented by Vienna chefs, and shaped and named after the Turkish symbol, the crescent. Thus Viennese forever consume their foe.

We can't even escape our eponyms by lighting up with an after-dinner cigarette. Jean Nicot (1530-1600) a French diplomat, while in Lisbon, was given some seeds of a rare plant that had recently been shipped from America. He thus brought tobacco to France and is duly remembered for its highly toxic constituent, **nicotine**. To think that nicotine is also used as an insecticide may prove so upsetting, you might want to forget this whole affair, including the bill.

But not so fast. You may become **dunned**, thanks to Joe Dun, a bailiff of Lincoln (England) during the reign of Henry VII, whose relentless and vigorous pursuit of deadbeats landed him in the annals of etymological history. ❧

†See "Stretching a Point"
* See "Old Soldiers Never Die: Eponyms II"
‡ See "Spreading a Little Salt Around"
** See "Flows the Don"

Euphemistically Speaking

A N ENGLISH KING NEVER lost his head at the fall of a guillotine. That's too barbaric. He was shorn of crown. Skunk pelts, when first marketed, were positioned as Alaskan sable, an attempt to avoid the negative association of an odor fouling sales.

Our habit of softening the harsh or unpleasant into more palatable expressions is so pervasive that the Greeks long ago gave us a word for it ... **euphemism,** from **eu** (good) and **phemi** (speak).

Perhaps one of the most common euphemisms is the term "passed away" in lieu of the stark "died." Another way of mitigating the shattering realism of dying is to shift the focus to the survivors, as in "We lost Barbara." A hospital doesn't lose patients during surgery. But it does own up to "involuntary conversions."

The concept of pregnancy gave birth to all kinds of euphemistical expressions. Among them: She's in a family way, in a delicate condition, well-along, expecting, about to have a blessed event, and the slang expression, she has a cake in the oven.

Only the ribald would refer to a whorehouse. More acceptable is the house of prostitution or brothel. Still more euphemistic are the terms sporting house, disorderly house or house of ill-repute.

Except in medical surroundings we indeed would raise eyebrows expressing the need to have a bowel movement or to urinate. Expressions to satisfy our penchant for verbally dodging this bit of biological reality abound. Hence we go to the powder room, privy, latrine, comfort station, rest room, biffy, wash room, water closet, lavatory, men's or women's room.

The crapper may in some circles dubiously qualify as a euphemism. It supposedly honors Sir Thomas Crapper, an English sanitary engineer and inventor of the flush-toilet, but the eponym is crap, or nonsense. The word **crap** predates the man and derives from the Dutch **krappe,** which denotes straw when it becomes mixed with dung when used to sweep the latter from barns.

Automobile dealers think we prefer to buy previously owned vehicles, in lieu of used cars. Garbage collectors are fast becoming extinct in favor of less offensive waste management and sanitation companies.

No longer do some companies announce a layoff upon a downturn in business. Instead these organizations undergo scheduled adjustments due to downsizing or "rightsizing." The individual employee caught up in all this is "excessed" or "transitioned." This verbal garbage might sound better to management than the harsh truth that it goofed by over expanding. But it offers scant comfort to the "dehired" who know they have been fired.

Our inclination to shed a better light on the dark side of events is exemplified at all levels of government. Raising taxes is suicidal for politicians. But we are faced with revenue enhancements . . . often in the form of user fees for services previously provided free. Our armed forces didn't parachute onto the island of Grenada. They were involved in a "predawn vertical insertion."

Long ago, we gave up insane asylums and jails. We now have mental institutions and correctional facilities.

The former Soviet Union had an interesting way of palatably handling references to more than a fifth of their population that live at or near poverty levels. They, in Soviet-speak, are "underprovisioned."

The financial community is replete with euphemistic expressions. Our Federal Reserve, for example, is often characterized as accommodative. De-euphemized, it simply opened up the money spigot or pushed interest rates lower by reducing the discount rate to member banks, hopefully not enough to invite inflation. Conversely, it can be restrictive, that is reduce the money supply or cause interest rates to rise, hopefully not enough to cause a recession.

It was the English, however, not the Greeks, that gave us **euphuism,** often confused with euphemism. The former refers to Euphues, the main character of several works by a 14th-century author, John Lyly. Lyly's extremely verbose prose was marked by alliterations and figures of speech. Hence his style, which supposedly influenced others, including Shakespeare, was dubbed **euphuistic.** ⁊

Digitalis: How and Why

ONE DEFINITION OF **DIGITALIS,** a myocardial arrest preventive, epitomizes the rich heritage of the English language. Digitalis, Latin for fingers, metaphorically could be named for its massage-like effect of fingers stimulating heart muscles. Sounds plausible, but untrue.

Rather, digitalis is an alternative name for the foxglove plant, the latter in turn from **fingerhut.** Foxglove was contrived by the

Germans in the 1500s, and inspired by the plant's purplish flowers that mimic the shape of a finger, or digit, hence the Latin version digitalis. The **hut**, or hat, of fingerhut equates to a thimble in German, hence glove. Why **fox** precedes **glove** remains a mystery. One speculative explanation hinges on fox as a corruption of folks.

With English history replete with invasions, real or attempted, by numerous European adversaries, small wonder the worldly class of its language. For example, taking our digitalis definition one step further, myocardial is a combination of the Greek **mus**, for muscle, and **cardiacus** (Latin) or **cardiaque** (French) or **kardiakos** (Greek) . . . all pertaining to the heart.

We can thank the French for our **arrest**, their **arret**, in turn a descendent of Old French **arreste**. (Aside, the French apply their arret more broadly, to a stream of things or events in motion, as opposed to our more limited usage of arrest, as in stopping or legally apprehending. Their traffic jam, verbosely is "**arret de la circulation**," or a straight-through flight, "**trajet sans arret**.") Therefore we use Latin, Greek, French, and German to define digitalis . . . not a word native to English.

The herb's medicinal magic is as interesting as its etymology. It's made from dried, powdered foxglove leaves, which contain digitoxin, a crystalline steroid, which stimulates the heart muscle, usually within a half-to-two hours after taken.

It can help fight off heart failure by improving the deteriorated pumping function of a heart whose muscles contain scar tissue, in turn caused by high blood pressure. Underlying reasons for the abnormal blood pressure vary: smoking, obesity, diabetes, metabolic diseases, etc. Digitalis, benignly, makes the healthy part of the heart muscle work harder to compensate for the lack of pumping action by the scar tissue.

It's suspected that digitalis's potential chemical energy is converted to mechanical energy by a series of processes in which calcium ions enter heart muscle cells while the cell membranes are temporarily depolarized by the clever digitalis. The result: Heart chamber fibrillation adjusts to a more normal and regular rhythm.

We originally "took the tincture of Digitalis" in the late 1700s, thanks to the discovery of its medicinal value by the British. Despite a plethora of advances in pharmacology in the succeeding 200 years, the powder and power of foxglove remain a viable medicine, widely prescribed by physicians, to control improperly pulsating heart muscles. All this assumes, of course, that digitalis is properly prescribed and ingested . . . else one runs the risk of becoming "digitized," as in the statistical sense. ᴥ

Ore Lore

R ANCH HANDS FORSOOK their cattle, seamen abandoned their ships, soldiers deserted their ranks, and storekeepers left their shops. From around the world they came to California to pan the rivers and then dredge them with boat-laden chain buckets, to pound the hard granite with hammer and chisel, break it up with pneumatic drills, blast it with dynamite and eventually to raze entire mountain sides with powerful jets of water. Gold was the lure. But more was discovered; the miner's tailings revealed a rich lode of legend and lore.

First pickings were easy. One simply panned a **placer**, that is sand and gravel deposits along a river bank. As the pan was artfully rocked by the prospector, the weight of the gold (almost twice that of lead, for example) caused it to settle to the bottom of the pan while lighter materials washed out.

Once California achieved statehood in 1850, an act hastened by the gold rush and over the objections of southern slave states, gold was cast into bars for delivery to the US Mint in San Francisco. The end product was an 89-pound brick. So much, and too much, for the Hollywood version of the stagecoach hijacker tossing with one hand gold bars into leather sacks and then nonchalantly slinging them over the back of his horse.

Back to placer. It stretches far back as a flat **place**, per the I-E **pla**, thence to the Roman **planus** and the Greek **platus**. Its meaning gradually widened with the Latin **platea**, a wide street, and the Greek **plateia**, a public place or square. Hence plazas world-wide with the Italian **piazza**, Spanish **plaza** and German **Platz**, all city squares. It's the Spanish plaza, eventually **placel** and its variant placer, that gave us a special place, that is the sandbank and mining sense. Placer deposits also are referred to as **alluvial**, from the Latin **alluvium**, a deposit created by flowing water. Alluvium flows from **luere**, the combining form of **lavere**, to wash. Hence the **lavatory**.

The settlement of Dry Diggings, so disrupted with placer mining scars, was renamed with its present appellation **Placerville** in 1850. However, in those times it was more renowned for its soubriquet **Hangtown**, a result of summary hangings from a giant oak next to the Placer Hotel. If you don't object to cholesterol-rich food, California gold country chefs still respond to requests for Hangtown fries with a time-honored amalgamation of fried eggs, oysters and bacon. Legends conflict whether the dish, an expensive one in gold rush days, owes its heritage to a miner with a suddenly fattened poke or the last request of a condemned.

(Substantiating that even words of gold were highly coveted, Placerville is not the seat of Placer County, that honor belonging to Auburn, one county to the north. Placerville, however, is the seat of **El Dorado** County, nevertheless spawned of gold lore. El Dorado, the gilded one in Spanish, originally was the name ascribed to the king of the city of Manoa, located on the Amazon, reputedly surrounded with so much gold that the king there was smothered in oil and continuously powdered with gold dust. Hence El Dorado applies to a place of wealth, despite unsuccessful attempts by Spanish conquistadores and England's Sir Walter Raleigh to find the apparently mythical kingdom.)

Once the easy placer pickings of flakes and occasional nuggets were exhausted, miners directed their efforts to the placer's mother veins. This was hard-rock mining, unquestionably hard work. Manually chiseling quartz-bearing gold out of granite was known as **jacking**. For two dollars per day jackers worked in tunnels "so much lower than their heads they had to crawl in and double up like **jack knives**."

The jacker's pay, however, was the envy of the **mucker**, who for a dollar a day loaded mining carts with waste material or **muck**. In a frenzied peak of activity a mucker could load a ton of muck in ten minutes! He owes his derogative title to the Middle English **muc**, the Old Norse **myki**, or cow **dung**. The mucker's day was not done, though, without attending to dung in the true sense. Mules were employed to pull mining carts along horizontal tunnels. Some 357 miles of them, connecting vertical shafts as deep as a mile beneath the surface, still exist at the Empire Mine in Grass Valley.

So essential were mules that mistreating them was sure grounds for dismissal. Skilled Cornish immigrants, who brought their hard-rock expertise from England's impoverished economy, quickly learned how to motivate mules. With tobacco! Try passing a mule in a narrow tunnel and a mucker would likely be pinned to a rock by the mule's powerful body until appropriate toll was paid with a plug.

Rough work required tough clothing. And the miner's apparel, though American made, had international roots of German ingenuity, French cloth, and Italian and Indian craftsmanship.

Levi Strauss, a Bavarian immigrant via New York City, was astute in realizing the miners need for dry goods, a demand magnified by most clothing merchants closing their shops and heading for Sierra pay dirt.

Strauss landed in San Francisco in 1853 with a supply of brown canvas for making tents, but soon learned by talking with miners that their most pressing need was rugged trousers. When his supply of brown canvas ran out, he switched to a cloth from Nimes, France, **serge de Nimes,** later compressed into what we know as **denims,** and in the familiar blue color. Copper rivets, added later, served a practical purpose beyond simply appearance. Strength they added to the pockets helped preclude their tearing when loaded with ore samples.

Long before similar garments were known as **jeans,** anglicized from the cloth of **Genoa.** And a coarse calico, woven cloth from **Dungri,** India became known as **dungarees.** And, of course, we must add to this list, what is the most popular name for these trousers (just ask any school kid, worldwide) the venerable **Levi's.**®

High-grading, smuggling ore from a mine, was grounds for immediate dismissal. Taking mine dung home, ostensibly for a garden, served as an ideal conduit for high-grading by an enterprising Empire Mine mucker, until his boss discovered the garden was nonexistent.

The streets of nearby Nevada City (California) were paved with gravel tailings of the Empire Mine, and thus with traces of gold. Thanks to the gold rush the streets of San Francisco were built of garbage. Piers projected out from what is now Montgomery Street and the heart of the financial district. Ships docked there (500 of them by 1850) and abandoned by gold-seeking crews became brothels, bars, and gambling dens. Eventually the ships and their flotsam became bay-fill extensions to city streets. The scenario aptly spawned a limerick:

The miners came in forty-nine
The prostitutes in fifty-one
And then they got together
And produced the native son.

San Francisco Bay was not the only environmental casualty of the gold rush. Older river beds of gold-encrusted quartz and deep gravel placers, entombed near bedrock by millions of years of geological forces that created the Sierra Nevada range, were beyond the miner's pan, but not his ingenuity. Enter the **monitor**, from the Latin **monere**, to warn, advise. This sense makes a lot of sense as in the name of the Union ironclad warship with its rotating turret of fire power, as the crew of the Confederate Merrimac learned.

The tapered nozzle used in hydraulic mining shifts monitor to a more reactive sense, a device for observation and detection. It enabled crews to direct water pressure with precision and to ascertain quickly their progress in dislodging boulders and dirt surrounding a hidden placer.

Obtaining water pressure was another matter. To satisfy the thirst of Malakoff Diggins, just north of Nevada City, water was diverted through miles of **flumes**, artificial water ways, from the Latin **flumen** (stream). Amazingly a 40-mile ditch, an 8,000-foot tunnel through solid bedrock, a dam with a capacity of one billion cubic feet of water and **sluice** boxes hundreds of feet in length, among other "improvements" were primarily built manually, with shovel and pick. The end result enabled Malakoff crews to work nearly 100,000 tons of gravel daily!

The quartz, gravel and muck blasted out were directed through sluice boxes, from the Latin **exclusus**, past participle of **excludere**, to **exclude**. The heavier gold was excluded from muck by **riffles** affixed to the bottom of the sluices. Riffle here carries the same sense of our riffling a stack of letters to find a coveted envelope containing a check, while ignoring those with bills.

The pit at Malakoff created by hydraulic mining measures approximately 7,000 feet by 1,000 feet and is up to 600 feet deep in places. Tons of tailings silted the Yuba River, inundating and destroying downstream farms, flooding Marysville, impairing navigation all the way to San Francisco and closing off channels to steamboat traffic. Levees were built continuously higher in the bay's delta. So some experts speculate, a gigantic 4-mile by 2,000-foot bar about 10 miles outside the Golden Gate probably was created by silt flowing from hydraulic mining. It's still a continuous trap for sediment that flows out of the delta because of reduced flushing power from the demand and divergence of water from the delta. Annually the Corps of Engineers must dredge the center of the bar to clear the main shipping channel into the bay, a perennial testimony due in part to California's freewheeling hydraulic mining era.

Essays have been written on **assayers** and their malicious promotion of mining stocks. Assay, the examination of ore to determine its quantity of gold or silver, evolved from the Middle French essay, a literary composition in current usage, but one that can be a trial or an examination. The French got their idea for **essayer** from the Late Latin **exagium, exigere,** to examine. Exigere also is a progenitor of our **exact,** a characteristic often shared by assayers and essayists.

Many a crooked assayer lived by the golden rule: They who hath the gold make the rules. Accordingly they helped like-minded mine developers promote a **borrasca,** Spanish for unfavorable weather and an allusion to a worthless mine, as a **bonanza,** Spanish for good sailing weather and an allusion to the good luck of developing a productive mine.

Mark Twain in his *Roughing It* tells of assayers weary of losing business to an extremely successful competitor suspected of salting mines to help owners artificially boost the price of their mining stock. The honest assayers sent a chip from a carpenter's grindstone to their suspect for an assay and received a glowing report of a predicted yield of almost $1300 of silver and $365 of gold per ton of ore! The sham was immediately publicized and the offending assayer run out of town.

Eureka! California's motto, recognizes the discovery of Archimedes, a Greek philosopher, mathematician and inventor (2nd century BC) who was pressed into service as one of the world's early assayers. He faced the challenge of testing Syracusan King Hiero's crown to determine if its gold was pure or alloyed with silver. So the story goes, while getting into his bathtub Archimedes noticed that the water was overflowing the side of the tub. That observation sparked a methodology for testing the crown: Simply stated, a body displaces its own weight in water. Eureka, he cried . . . from the Greek **heureka**: I have found (it). Excited, he ran home without taking time to don his clothes. There he found that by so testing the crown in water in comparison with pure gold and silver, it was, as the king suspected, deficient. This also explains why educators refer to **heuristic** teaching as a method wherein students are encouraged to find solutions themselves.

Heuristic learning aside, linguistically it took us awhile to categorize gold's brilliance as **yellow**. The I-E **gold**, that is **gholt**, **ghel**, gave way to numerous offshoots including the Germanic **gelo**, **gel**, which became the Old English **geolo** and Middle English **yelwe, yelow**. The lightness of the heavy metal dawned upon the Romans long before. Their gold, or **aurum**, is akin to **Aurora**, their goddess of the dawn, and as a result our symbol, **Au**, for gold.

"I never knew but one woman who would not take gold, and she took diamonds," said Horace Walpole, underscoring our penchant for gold. In the form of jewelry, gold's value can be perplexing, a matter that takes us to the Mediterranean and the **carob** trees that flourish there. Their seeds or **carats**, so it was reasoned, weighed approximately the same as the smallest of gemstones. Thus the weight of precious stones and metals became carat equivalents. Eventually (in the early 20th century) a carat was standardized more definitively at 200 milligrams. Carat stems from the Arabic **qirat** or carob bean.

Confounding all this, the carat was once used to designate the amount of pure gold in alloy. Fortunately this evolved to **karat,** at units of 1/24. Hence 18-karat gold is alloyed with 6 karats of another metal. All this perhaps proves that one doesn't know beans, if not a carat from a karat.

"Boys, I believe I have **found** a gold mine," said James Marshall upon noticing yellowish flecks in a tailrace he had deepened to improve the operation of a water-powered saw mill along the American River's south fork in Colma Valley. With that **profound** observation, one of the world's worst kept secrets, despite intentions otherwise of Marshall and his partner John Sutter, California's gold rush began.

It's believed that the I-E root **gheu, kheu,** to pour, led to the Latin **fundere,** to pour or shape by melting. This artistry was picked up in Old French as **fondre,** which gave English its **foundry,** a facility for casting gold.

Fundere poured out all kinds of **confounding** compounds, among them this adjective that literally denotes a pouring together of perplexing or bewildering elements. A few of the other relatives in the fundere family include such disparities as **font,** printer's type that once was cast in metal; the adjective **effusive,** our form of **efundere,** a pouring out of emotions or demonstrative reaction; and even a **refund,** based upon **refundere,** literally an act of pouring back.

And while we are at it, **fusion.** It could be a melting of different political positions. It could be a thermonuclear reaction of light atoms joining to form heavier atoms, or a transmutation of base metals into noble gold.

All this fundere should not be confused with another founding, the Latin **fundare,** probably a descendent of the I-E **bhund,** to base firmly. This family and its derivatives served as a **foundation** for many base words, including **funds**, as in those **fundamental** resources and the money required to start up a mining venture.

Finding gold has been a more successful venture than creating it, a perennial but frustrating goal of the **alchemists**, whence our modern **chemists**. They have been at it for several millennia. The Old French had its **alquemie**, borrowed from the Roman's **alchymia**, in turn the Arabic **alkimiya**. That's a composite of the Arabic **al** (the) plus **kimiya**, from the Greek **kemeia**, meaning a **transmutation**, or change (the Latin **mutare**) of one substance into another.

Etymologists have suggested in a somewhat nebulous scenario that the root of all this is the Greek **Chymeia**, their word for Egypt, in turn from **Kym**, the Egyptian god of the Nile. As the Nile flows forth, so does the Greek **chein** mean to pour. All of this pouring, along with smelt-mixing of base metals, sparked the alchemists imagination that somehow gold could magically result.

Though fusion someday may prove him right, all that glittered turned out not to be gold for the alchemist. So true, too, for Marshall and Sutter. Sutter once was wealthy, owning not only his sawmill, but much more valuable vast land holdings via a Mexican land grant. Prospectors from around the world prowled over his land staking claims. Turning to the military to assert his rights in what was then a US settlement was fruitless. Many soldiers were busy staking their claims, probably on Sutter's disputed land. For nine years he petitioned Congress to recognize his land claims that were invalidated by the US Supreme Court. He died bankrupt in 1880 in Washington DC, the day after Congress adjourned, once more failing to restore his questionable land rights.

Marshall's later years as a carpenter, vintner, rancher and once more prospector were unrewarding. Rumors of heavy drinking followed him. In an appearance to obtain renewal of a pension from the California legislature in 1878, a bottle of brandy is reputed to have fallen from his jacket and rolled across the floor. Pension denied. He died seven years later. ✒

Crux Matters

W E SAIL ACROSS THE sea, bear onerous burdens, engage in our most popular parlor pastime, devour nutritious vegetables, embark on a cause with zeal, recognize neutrality, sign documents and once even settled judicious disputes simply because of one of our most ubiquitous symbols . . . the **cross**. It symbolizes the best and the worst in the character of man. Bearing it, we kill, we protect.

What once denoted a post supporting a beam, the Latin **crux**, became a handy device of torture, specifically for **crucifying** one . . . crux plus the Latin **figere**, to fasten. Thus the crucifixion of Jesus Christ at the hands of Pontius Pilate. Crux also became the Late Latin and English cross. Hence our allusion to **bearing a cross** when faced with heavy burdens.

And therein lies the crux sense of our matters, the puzzlement when solutions escape us. "Whoever takes up the sword shall perish by the sword. And whoever does not take up the sword (or lets it go) shall perish on the cross," per Simone Weil, succinctly illustrates the problem.

We perpetuated the icon of the cross of Christ and Christianity in early English classes by placing a cross-lined symbol at the start of the alphabet in spelling books. The gradual loss of its religious significance in spellers and the eventual spelling of **Christ('s) cross** yielded the term **crisscross**.

Christ's name, however, was literally ground from the seeds of oil. **Chrism**, a consecrated oil used in church rites, evolved from the Old English **crisma**, previously the Late Latin **chrisma**, equivalent to the Greek **khrismsa**, an anointing oil, thanks in turn to the Greeks and their **khriein**, to rub, anoint. They got this idea from the Sanskrit **gharsati**, meaning "he rubs, grinds," as one does oil from seeds. Even speakers of Sanskrit in India can't claim originality here. They probably took their cue from the I-E root **ghrei**, to rub, grind.

It can be presumed that indeed Christ was **charismatic**, having the God-given power to perform miracles. Any connection of this characteristic with the crisma base of his name, however, is linguistic heresy. **Charisma**, first recorded in the 17th century, stems from the Greek **charizesthai**, to show favor, grace and is akin to **chairein**, rejoice. The latter, etymologists suggest, probably is from the Greek **kharis**, God-given grace, in turn the I-E **gher** (desire) which rubs close, but not close enough to ghrei.

Back to the Greek khriein. Its past participle **khristos** evolved to **Kristos** (the Anointed One) and the Late Latin **Christus**, our Christ. His followers, **Christians**, similarly stem from the Greek and Latin **khristianos, christianus**.

In the name of Christianity mankind suffered the **crusades**, wherein many indeed did die by the sword. Eight distinct wars were waged by Europeans between the 11th and 13th centuries to recapture the Holy Land from Mohammedan conquerors.

Soldiers assumed that "God wills it" after a pep talk from Pope Urban II in 1095. But it probably never crossed their minds that when wearing the cross they were an easily identified target for their foes. The French had a verb for it: **Croiser**, to take up the cross of a crusader. The French, however, share credit with the Spanish for crusader. The Latin crux became the Old French **crois** and **croisade**. Not to be out-dueled in the war of words, the Spanish invented **cruzada**. Thus our crusade is a blend of the Spanish prefix **cru-** plus the French suffix **-sade**.

We would be stretching our credulity to regard a ship-borne crusader crossing the Mediterranean as on a **cruise**. Literally, though, he is. Cruise hails from the old crux, which the Dutch picked up as **kruis, kruisen** and extended its concept of one stick crossing another to a ship crossing a body of water.

A crossing of the Rubicon by Caesar in 49 BC left us an indelible aphorism. Weary of Caesar's growing power as occupier and governor of Cisalpine Gaul, the senate in his mother country ordered his return to Rome, but without his army, a condition he was loath to accept. The seriousness of disobeying the senate weighed heavily upon him. According to the Greek biographer Plutarch, Caesar dreamt the night prior to taking this war-like action that he had intercourse with his mother, an illusion Freudians later could explain. Once his military decision was made Caesar proclaimed, **Iacta alea est,** "the die is cast." Hence when we **cross a Rubicon,** we embark upon a hazardous and irrevocable undertaking.

Now we have expanded our concept of crusade to any cause undertaken with zeal, a sense probably first proposed by Thomas Jefferson when he implored, "Preach, my dear Sir, a crusade against ignorance." Certainly grounded in ignorance was the custom of **judgment by the cross.** Under Charlemagne, King of the Franks (8th century) plaintiffs and defendants of a dispute would undergo a perseverance contest requiring them to keep their arms folded **across** their chests. The last to give up this rigid posture prevailed.

With both zeal and ignorance mercenaries of Rome engaged in a 13th-century European crusade against peaceful Christian heretics. Monks offered papal remission of sins for volunteering 40 days of service in a holy war that eventually eliminated the Cathars, who resided in the Languedoc and **Albigensian** (people of **Albi**[†]) regions of Southern France. The penalty for not buying Rome's line was death. In some instances chained prisoners were marched into a pyre and burned alive. If a soldier could not distinguish a Catholic from a heretic, he was instructed to kill anyway, as God would sort it all out later.

As a prelude to death many victims were blinded, their noses cut off, their tongues cut out. Stupidity reigned on both sides. Many Cathars deceived themselves into believing that death by fire was beautiful. Some were granted this wish posthumously, their mutilated bones exhumed, then burned in a public ceremony by those wearing the cross.

More humane compassion for prisoners in contemporary times is symbolized by the **Red Cross**. Founded in 1864 in Geneva, Switzerland (also the base of approximately 150 other international organizations) the Red Cross appropriately reflects neutrality, as does its host country in modern times. Fittingly the organization's red cross on a white background mimics the country's **white cross** on red. Not all, however, was peaceful with the white cross. The symbol of Christian faith was adopted in the 11th century as a symbol of freedom by the canton of **Schwyz**, one of three founding cantons and inspiration for the name **Switzerland**. That action inspired soldiers of all succeeding cantons to wear crossed strips of white linen on their tunics or armor as a battle standard in the country's many medieval wars, alliances, mercenary adventures, internal disturbances and European revolutions, undertaken prior to its age of neutrality.

We can't even escape crosses when dining. Vegetables of the mustard family are classified as **cruciferous**, reflecting the overlapping or crossed appearance of their petals . . . cross plus **fer**, that which carries, from the Latin **ferre**, to bear. Some (just ask George Bush) bear a cross for broccoli, a cruciferous they find **excruciatingly** painful to contemplate, despite its highly touted nutritious value. These people suffer unbearably, as implied in **cruciare** is the original sense of torture, intensified by the prefix **ex**. It's wise not to force broccoli upon them. They may become snappish or cross, may even have **cross words** for you.

In a more pleasant vein this brings up what is portrayed as America's most popular indoor game, one enjoyed by more than 50 million devotees, the **crossword puzzle**. It requires a nimble mind, but also a nascent ability to write, to solve a crossword puzzle. This capability unfortunately escapes the illiterate, who have their cross to bear, but also their "X" to serve as a signature. &

†See "One Word Generates Another"

Whence Politico-Americana

AMERICA AND ITS POLITICS are products more of happenstance than design, a case of someone reaching up and grabbing an appellation at hand to unwittingly immortalize the country's heritage.

What was to become our manifest destiny was originally part of **Mundus Novus**, the New World. An Italian map maker and navigator, Amerigo Vespucci, who also served as a ship chandler for Columbus and made several voyages to the new world, so named it. But later a German geographer referred to the New World as America, an honor for Vespucci that obviously stuck. Perhaps we should be thankful. North New World doesn't have such a nice ring.

Of course, our precedents for misnomers start with Vespucci's boss, Columbus, who mistakenly thought he reached his Far East China-India destination when he waded ashore in the Bahamas and therefore called the natives **Indians**, hence the American

Indian. This also explains why the islands surrounding the Bahamas are known as the **West Indies.**

Our political labels are more complex. Generically our political organizations are aptly named **parties,** a word that owes its allegiance to the Old French **partie,** inspired by the Latin **pars.** This root in one sense means to divide, and in an other to contest, both ardent attributes of a party's office seekers whether dividing their party in a primary or the country in a final election. A later use of party was adopted for the sense of revelment by **participants** especially picked, or divided, for the purpose of a social occasion. This scene also depicts many a political convention when the nomination of a ticket is well assured beforehand through numerous primaries and caucuses.

In the dividing sense, the Democrats have been characterized by one American humorist (Peter Finly Dunne) as a "Party that ain't on speaking terms with itself." They nevertheless are a party to be reckoned. "Republicans sleep in twin beds–some even in separate bedrooms–and that's why there are more Democrats", is the rather stuffy characterization of these people, according to another observer, Will Stanton. Fittingly, so claim many Democrats, the name Republican bears a rather pompous origin.

Res publica, Latin for entity plus people, otherwise translates as affairs of state. Our Republicans are a reformed party of the **Whigs.** (This is not because they wore them. They were not that stuffy. The hairpiece **wig** is clipped from the French **periwig,** a ribbon that gathered a powdered wig behind the neck.)

Our colonial Whigs opposed royal governors and the latter's loyalty to the English crown. They appropriately borrowed the term from the British Whigs, who in 1689 formed a party to oppose the Tories, who supported the crown. Eventually the Whigs became Britain's liberal party.

Whig was pulverized from **Whiggamore,** meaning outlaws in Scotland. Presbyterians there earned this designation because in

1648 they raided Edinburgh to protest the succession of the Catholic Duke of York to the throne. Appropriately, whig is Scottish for spurring on, briskly, as presumably did many Presbyterians on their **mares.**

It's understandable that we never had a successful **Tory** party. "A Tory," according to one Whig, "is a thing whose head is in England, whose body is in America, and whose neck ought to be stretched." The Brits with their Whigs and Tories prove that many a dissident can be characterized as an outlaw. In 1646 Tory was a hypocritical term heaped upon Irish Catholics, who resorted to banditry after being dispossessed of their land, banned from selling their cattle to England and prevented from engaging in trade with the American colonies.

In 1689 the **Tories** formed a political party and later embraced anyone who supported the Catholic Duke of York (James II) as successor to the throne. In the early 19th century the Tories officially became the Conservative party, yet are still known as Tories, from the Irish **toruighe,** plunderer, descendant of the Old Irish **toirighim,** meaning "I pursue." This all brings to mind Ambrose Bierce's aside that, "A conservative is a statesman who is enamored of existing evils, as distinguished from the liberal who wishes to replace them with others."

Democrats find their etymological ancestry with the Greeks, via the French **democratie,** progeny of **demokratia,** a compounding of **demos** (people) plus **kratos** (power or rule). A cognate of demos is the Irish **dam,** meaning following a crowd, an aspiration our Democratic majority professes. A related word they certainly eschew is **demagogue,** a leader, **agogos,** of the people, now disparagingly a reference to an unprincipled leader who connivingly arouses the masses.

Democrats can tenuously claim they are the party of Jefferson, Madison, Monroe and John Quincy Adams, all who gained the presidency on tickets sponsored by the Democrat-Republican party, which by 1828 was reformed into the Democratic party.

Politicians claim astuteness at running our country, yet have proved inept at creating emblems representing their parties. What dyed-in-the-wool Democrat would claim an ass as a symbol, or one stupid, silly and obstinate? Yet all these characterizations are usages of the word **donkey.**

And the Republican party runs the risk of being branded as a **white elephant,** something most undesirable. Its genesis is found in Siamese folklore, wherein kings awarded disliked courtiers gifts of white elephants, because their reputed expensive upkeep would ruin the recipient.

Perhaps the party symbol that most reflects a desirable image, again an animal, is the **Bull Moose.** After serving most of the unfinished term of the assassinated McKinley and his own elected term, Teddy Roosevelt partook in a big game safari in Africa, leaving party leadership to his hand-picked successor, Willlam Howard Taft. Returning with a change of heart he challenged Taft's second term, but lost in the Republican convention. He then bolted the party with liberal Republicans to form the Progressive party. To allay any fears of his capacity to fight the big fight, Rooosevelt pronounced himself strong as a bull moose. Being a bull moose or bull-headed wasn't enough. In the election of 1911 Democrat Wilson prevailed over the Republican Taft, his party badly splintered by Roosevelt Progressives.

Parties and their candidates unceasingly contrive for our coveted **vote,** a concept even our I-E friends recognized in their **wegwh,** meaning to speak solemnly. That translated into the Latin **vovere,** to vow, later to wish, finally to do so with a vote.

The fair sex, until the 19th amendment was ratified in 1920, were unfairly denied the right to vote. **Suffer** the indignity they did, from the Latin **sufferre, suf** (a variant of sub, under) plus **ferre** (to bear). This bearing under, however, bears no etymological connection with woman's **suffrage,** advocated especially by **suffragettes.**

Suffrage is another Latin word for voting. It's borrowed from the Old French **suffrage** (prayers or pleas) based upon the Latin **suffragari,** to express support. You can almost hear the roar of support in their **fragor** (a breaking noise) plus suf (again, under), that is the noise of the crowd offering support from below.

One of the more devious schemes for capturing votes involves legislatures carving election districts in a manner that offers the party in power a majority of adherents in many districts while concentrating the strength of the opposition in a minimal number of districts. Credit for this political legerdemain goes to Governor Gerry Elbridge of Massachusetts, whose Democrat-Republican party redistricting efforts in 1812 appeared on maps to resemble the **meandering** shape of a **salamander.** The party won less popular votes than the opposing Federalists, but thanks to gerrymandering, won almost three times more seats than the Federalists to the state senate. As a result Gerry and salamander were convoluted into the compound **gerrymander,** now an eponymous noun. Ultimate and shared credit, however, goes back to the Greek **maiandros,** inspired by the **Menderes** River that winds across West Asia Minor into the Aegean Sea, thus giving gerrymander the distinction of a double eponym.

Political campaigns have boiled down to memorable slogans, e.g. "I like Ike." Another that rhythmically rolls off one's tongue was fashioned by the Whigs in the campaign of 1840. The party captured the glory of their candidate William Henry Harrison's defeat of the famed Indian warrior Chief Tecumseh at Tippecanoe River in Indiana by the catchy "Tippecanoe and Tyler, too." The Harrison-Tyler ticket threw out the incumbent Democrat Martin Van Buren, whom the Whigs labeled Martin Van Ruin. All this brings to mind some sage advice of Joe Cannon: "Sometimes in politics one must duel with skunks, but no one should be fool enough to allow the skunks to choose their weapons."

"**Politics** is perhaps the only profession for which no preparation is thought necessary", so observed Robert Louis Stevenson. In other words it makes strange postmasters. Eytmologically, however, it once shared the high ground. It invaded our lexicon from the Greek **polis,** city, thanks to the I-E **pel,** suspected to refer to a heaping up, as in a wall or fortress, thus the beginnings of the protection afforded by a city.

We have advanced this concept much further into **metropolises,** large cities, from the Greek **metropolis,** or mother city (**metro,** the combining form of **meter** or mother). Along the way we adopted politics and **politicians** who set **policy,** enforced, you guessed it, by the **police.**

Polite and **polish** also entered our lexicon as offsprings of the pel, or as the root germinated, the **pol** family. After all, politeness and polish are cultivated in an urbane environment, according to some devotees of etymology. That's rubbing polish the wrong way, say others. These dissenters claim both words descended from the French **polir,** the Latin **polire,** in turn **po, pro,** before, plus **lire,** from **linere,** to smear or rub, a prerequisite to something polished.

This all brings us back to Columbus. If Christopher had been more **politically** astute, he would have sought counsel and advice from the bronze man, discovered that he wasn't talking with Indians but with an aborigine from scores of **partitioned** tribes of new world natives.

The so-called Indian, who displayed politeness by greeting pilgrims with "Much welcome, Englishman" also showed polish by granting us one of our more enduring political institutions.[†] He gave us the **caucus,** from the Algonquian **caucauasu,** one who counsels and advises. ❧

[†] See "First Words"

Some Final Words

FINALITY COSTS. WE are very aware of this truism when faced with paying for a speeding ticket. More than a millennium ago the Romans taught us the realities of a **fine**, from their **finare**, to pay one. In so doing a dispute or a violation is **finalized**, all this because of their **finis**, passed on to us through the Old French **fin**, both meaning end, as a judge will so sanction.

Can we square the noun-verb fine we pay with the adjective we use to describe a fine lady, -wine, -day, or even fine gold in all its lustrous purity? The process of **refining** offers a hint. That's how we produce a host of commodities like sugar, metal and petroleum. It also equates to the more cerebric thoughts and images that dance around in the minds of writers and artists when refining their works. And it's the antithesis of vulgarity as displayed in refined taste.

What all these processes have in common, whether evidenced in the raw, flaming hot smelting of ore or the delicately balanced bouquet of a properly aged Chardonnay, is that each represents the outer limits of our knowledge and experience, the point where our state of the art ends.

Endings permeate our days. We often break off a visit or a phone conversation with a **good-bye**. Good-bye tilts toward a negative or somewhat sad connotation, compared with the more upbeat, expectant 'til-we-meet-again sense of the French **au revoir** and German **wiedersehen**. However, if we go back far enough, the 16th century, we can levitate good-bye to a more positive plane. When invoking it we were wishing our audience pious protection. Good-bye is a descendent and a contraction of **God be with you,** not exclusively an English expression, as evidenced by the French **adieu, a** (to) plus **dieu** (God), the Spanish **adios** and the Latin **ad deum.**

Farewell is more correctly uttered upon embarking on a journey . . . to go, or to travel, one of its many meanings handed down from the Old English **faran**. There's ample logic for the suffixal -well. **Travelling** once indeed was extremely dangerous, subject to the hazards of treacherous highwaymen, dangerous beasts, strange diseases, unreliable vehicles, unforgivable terrain, as well as the capriciousness of the weather. Such arduous undertakings explain why travel originally meant to labor and is a relative of **travail**, both offsprings of the Old French **traveillier**. The Romans started all of this with still another relative, their Vulgar Latin **tripaliare**: to torture, a characterization many a modern suburbanite applies to his daily commute. All this makes it abundantly clear, then and now, that whether traversing the Roman Via Salaria or the San Francisco-Oakland Bay Bridge, it's comforting to have God on your side.

It would be silly to sign off a letter "Without wax." But then again, some etymologists claim that's exactly what we do. And they are not referring to our intention of not sealing the envelope. **Sincerely** represents the thoughts of our letter as candid,

honest, perhaps heart-felt. Literal speculation characterizes our words as pure, unadulterated.

It's a case of **lucus a non lucendo**, literally a grove of trees created from darkness, that is without light (lucendo) . . . not a likely occurrence, hence this Roman expression for a false or questionable etymology as well as a means of palming off what isn't as what is.

To shed some light, that is **elucidate** (a cousin of lucendo with a common ancestor in the Latin root **luc**, or light) the questionable etymology of sincere, we turn to a devious ploy involving potters. An honest craftsman represents his pottery as **sine** (without) **cera** (wax). All this because such a substance was used by a crafty craftsman not only to put a false luster on his vase, but to fill the cracks and hide imperfections. You might say in his subtle, skillful ways that he **finessed** the sale of his work, ennobling it with a deceptive sense of **fineness**.

Other versions construct sincere from sine (without) plus the English **caries** (decay), suggesting purity, as well as **sym** (together) plus **crescare** (to grow), again implying purity, as we do with the words and thoughts of our correspondence.

When without luc, that is at day's end, especially in medieval times, we could be faced with a **curfew**. During government-declared emergencies or in periods of political unrest, the curfew cleared the streets, relegated us to our homes. However, with the original Old French **covrefeu** it was time to put out the fire at home. Fear of an individual fire igniting a conflagration inspired the curfew, from the Latin **covir** (cover) plus **feu** (fire).

In trying to conclude the tasks of a busy day, we often admit to being at loose ends. No more so than economists, of whom Bernard Shaw has observed, if they all were laid end-to-end, they would never reach a **conclusion**. A concluded subject is **closed**, as revealed in its Latin ancestor **claudere**, to close, plus **con**, to intensify the matter, in turn a descendent of the I-E **kleu**, a hook or peg, which closes, or at least grasps something. . . a sharp contrast to **enclosing** an armful of nothing when trying to peg our economist.

We also are at loose ends over the Latin **terminus**. The latter represents the end of practically anything, including **terms**, that is conditions. Recently brought to light are term limits many of the electorate wish to impose on their political representatives, on the theory that it is best to install a new set of bunglers in office before the old ones become too proficient at bilking their constituency.

The Romans **defined Terminalia** as a festival in February

wherein the **confines**, or limits, of their boundary stones were decorated with garlands and blessed with prayers. If you think this was an excuse for another grand Roman orgy, you are absolutely right. Terminalia wound up with an almost **infinite** variety of entertainment, and an abundance of wine, song, and food, all **climaxed** in mass love-making.

Climax eminently qualifies as a final word, whether the final act of sex, a play or musical score. This culmination of events, however, owes its heritage to a plain, old, tangible household item, the **ladder**. It's an outgrowth of the Greek **klimax**, a ladder and subsequently that last rung, which one reaches **climactically**.

Underscoring the cross-breeding of our words, climax has lots to do with our weather, and not because some storms may end only after a climatic cloud burst. Stripped of complexities, the story unfolds thusly. The Greek klimax, or ladder, is related to **kleinen**, to lean, and **klimat**, a slope . . . logical enough, as a ladder leans, slopes. This gives us an excuse to lean, as do we as **clients** when leaning on purveyors for their services. As to the weather, the Greeks leaned on the idea that the earth sloped towards the North Pole, a slippery premise from whence they perceived the cause of weather conditions.

Romans were adept at finding ladders to climb. Our **saturnalia**, unrestrained revelry, dates back to their festival of the same name. The god of the harvest, **Saturnus**, was honored with a week-long festival, climaxed with the usual merry-making, but also a time when schools were closed and prisoners freed. Add to this Terminalia, Lupercalia[†] plus numerous other celebrations and we understand the source of the Roman expression **plures cradula quam gladius**: drunkenness (kills) more than the sword.

With that terminating and logical thought let's turn to the illogic of the bus-air-railroad **terminal**, a designation that acknowledges only the destination of a trip and not the origin, possibly because our tortured traveler of yesteryear was so happy and relieved to get there.

Words, too, have origins, reflecting the aspirations and experiences of those who concoct them. They serve their terms, some **expiring**, literally a breathing out (**ex**) of their last **breath**, from the Latin **spirare**, to breathe. Others totter close to the abyss of extinction . . . as does **wer**, once a proud male, but now confined only to **werewolf**.

Many a word emeritus . . . whilst, thou, me-thinks . . . to name a few, rise into the **archaic**, a classification with oxymoronic[†] undertones. It harkens a beginning, but also an ending. The age of an **arch**,[**] whether a -bishop or a -duke, qualifies him as one who began his career first, and perhaps will end it first, in contrast to his peers.

Like the people who speak them, our world of words continues to expand. Borrowed from various cultures they are blended, compounded, coined, contrived into acronyms, "eponymized," depreciated, meliorated, replicated, clipped, back-formed, and in numerous other ingenious ways **originated**.

Thus, this, a beginning of an end, and with some license an end to a beginning, harkens back to its beginning, the **Origin** in its title, a story in itself. **Oriri**, to rise in Roman times gave us the **Orient**, as the sun rises from the east . . . that's toward the Orient from a European perspective. We became **oriented**, that is familiar with our surroundings and circumstances, by recognizing the east from the rising sun when we rose in the morning.

Navigators are preoccupied with becoming oriented. Before becoming attracted by the magnetics of a compass, navigators placed east at the top of their maps. Even churches predominantly faced eastward toward Jerusalem, a ray of light, orienting sailors just off-shore on a cloudy, sun-blocked day.

And hopefully, all this potpourri elucidates for you the fascinating origins of words wifs and wers have contrived.

[†] See "Culinary Concoctions: Eponyms III"
[*] See "Familiar Relations"
[‡] See "A Saying Before," "One Word Generates Another"
[**] See "Ships Of State," "Behind Those Titles"

❧ SELECT BIBLIOGRAPHY ❧

Sources employed for writing *Words* are rather extensive and to reference them throughout the text would be cumbersome for author and reader alike. Therefore direct quotations are attributed in the text while other more general sources are included in this bibliography.

The definitions and etymologies referred to in *Words* are not detailed, but rather are limited in scope to support the book's stories. Complete semantics as well as the etymological trails of words are the province respectively of dictionaries and dictionaries of etymology. Particularly recommended for those wishing to pursue either avenue further, and most helpful in the preparation of this book, are the dictionaries listed below. Equal appreciation is also due to the various other fine resources contained in the listing.

Auden, W.H. & Louis Kronenberger, *The Viking Book of Aphorisms: A Personal Selection.* Dorset Press by arrangement with The Viking Press, 1966.

Bartlett's Familiar Quotations. Emily Morrison Beck, Editor. Boston: Little, Brown And Company, 1980.

Barnhart, Robert K. *The Barnhart Dictionary of Etymology: The Core Vocabulary Of Standard English.* New York: The H. W. Wilson Company, 1988.

Beeching, Cyril Leslie. *A Dictionary of Eponyms.* Oxford: Oxford University Press, 1988.

Benet's Third Edition Reader's Encyclopedia. Carol Cohen, Editor. New York: Harper & Row, 1987.

Brewer's Dictionary of Phrase & Fable. Ivor H. Evans, Editor. London: Cassell Publishers, 1989.

Browning, D.C. *The Complete Dictionary of Shakespeare Quotations.* New York: New Orchard Editions, 1986.

Browning, D.C. *Dictionary of Quotations and Proverbs: A Comprehensive Collection Of Sayings, Quotations, Slogans and Proverbs.* Secaucus, New Jersey: Chartwell Books, Inc., 1982.

Bryson, Bill. *The Mother Tongue: English & How It Got That Way.* New York: William Morrow & Company, Inc., 1990.

Cassell's French Dictionary: French-English, English-French. Denis Girard, Editor. New York: Macmillan, 1981.

Cassell's German Dictionary: German-English, English-German. Harold T. Betteridge, Editor. New York: Macmillan, 1978.

Cassell's Italian Dictionary: Italian-English, English-Italian. Piero Rebora, Editor. New York: Macmillan, 1967.

Cassell's Latin Dictionary: Latin-English, English-Latin. D.P. Simpson, Editor. New York: Macmillan, 1968.

Ciardi, John. *A Browser's Dictionary: A Compendium of Curious Expressions & Intriguing Facts.* New York: Harper & Row, 1980.

Ciardi, John. *Good Words to You: An All-New Browser's Dictionary and Native's Guide To The Unknown American Language.* New York: Harper & Row, 1987.

Cuddon, J.A. *A Dictionary of Literary Terms.* New York: Penguin Books, 1987.

Claiborne, Robert. *The Roots of English: A Reader's Handbook Of Word Origins.* New York: Times Books, 1989.

Claiborne, Robert. *Loose Cannons and Red Herrings: A Book Of Lost Metaphors.* New York: Ballantine Books, 1988.

Davis, Kenneth C. *Don't Know Much About History: Everything You Need To Know About American History But Never Learned.* New York: Crown, 1990.

De Quille, Dan. *The Big Bonanza.* Las Vegas: Nevada Publications, 1974.

Dohlan, Mary Helen. *The Making of the American Language: From Its Anglo-Saxon Roots To The Modern Age.* New York: Dorset Press, 1974.

Dozier, Thomas A. *Whales & Other Sea Animals: Wild, Wild World of Animals.* Time-Life Films, Inc. 1977.

Edgar Allan Poe Stories . . . Twenty-Seven Thrilling Tales By The Master Of Suspense. Laura Benet, Editor. New York: Platt & Munk, 1961.

Ehrlich, Eugene. *Amo, Amos, Amot and More: How To Use Latin To Your Own Advantage And To The Astonishment Of Others.* New York: Harper & Row, 1985.

Encyclopaedia Britannica. London: Encyclopaedia Britannica, Inc. 1959.

Encyclopedia of the Third Reich. Snyder, Louis Leo. New York: McGraw-Hill, 1976.

Esar, Evan. *The Dictionary of Humorous Quotations.* New York: Dorset Press, 1949.

Fowler's Modern English Usage. Sir Ernest Gowers, Editor. Oxford: Oxford University Press, 1985.

Freeman, Morton S. *The Story Behind the Word.* Philadelphia: ISI Press, 1985.

Funk, Wilfred. *Word Origins: And Their Romantic Stories.* New York: Bell Publishing, 1978.

Green, Jonathon. *The Cynic's Lexicon.* New York: St. Martin's Press, 1984.

Gudde, Erwin G. *California Place Names.* Berkeley: University of California Press, 1969.

Gulland, Daphne M. and Hinds-Howell, David G. *The Penguin Dictionary of English Idioms.* London: Penguin Books, 1988.

Hanley, Cliff. *History of Scotland.* New York: Dorset Press, 1986.

Hendrickson, Robert. *The Ocean Almanac.* Garden City, New York: Doubleday & Company, 1984.

Laird, Charlton & Gorrell, Robert. *Reading about Language.* New York: Harcourt, Brace, Jovanovich, 1971.

Mackenzie, R.F. *A Search for Scotland.* London: William Collins, Sons, & Co., Ltd., 1989.

Macrone, Michael. *Brush Up On Your Shakespeare: An Infectious Tour Through The Most Famous And Quotable Words and Phrases From The Bard.* New York: Harper & Row, 1990.

Maleska, Eugene T. *A Pleasure in Words.* New York: Simon & Schuster, 1981.

McCrum, Robert; Cran, William; and MacNeil, Robert. *The Story of English.* New York: Viking Penguin, 1986.

McNamee, Laurence and Biffle, Kent. *A Few Words: A Cornucopia Of Questions And Answers Concerning Language, Literature, and Life.* Dallas: Taylor Publishing, 1988.

Metcalf, Fred. *The Penguin Dictionary of Modern Humorous Quotations.* New York: Viking, 1986.

Morris, Willam and Morris, Mary. *Morris Dictionary of Word Phrase Origins.* New York: Harper & Row, 1988.

Monterey Bay Aquarium. Monterey, CA.

The Oxford Dictionary of English Etymology. C.T. Onions, Editor. Oxford: Oxford University Press, 1966.

Oxford English Dictionary. James A. Murray, Editor. Oxford: The Claredon Press, 1844.

Paisner, Milton. *One Word Leads to Another: A Light History Of Words.* New York: Red Dembner Enterprises, 1982.

Partridge, Eric. *A Short Etymological Dictionary of Modern English.* New York: Greenwich House, 1983.

Partridge, Eric. *Smaller Slang Dictionary.* New York: Dorset Press, 1961.

Panati, Charles. *Extraordinary Origins of Everyday Things.* New York: Harper & Row, 1987.

Panati, Charles. *Browser's Book of Beginnings: Origins of Everything Under, And Including, The Sun.* Boston: Houghton Mifflin, 1984.

The Poems and Plays of Robert Browning. New York: Random House, 1934.

Rawson, Hugh. *A Dictionary of Euphemisms & Other Double-Talk.* New York: Crown, 1981.

Safire, William & Safir, Leonard. *Words of Wisdom: More Good Advice.* New York: Simon & Schuster, 1989.

Shipley, Joeseph T. *Dictionary of Word Origins.* New York: Philosophical Library, Inc., 1945.

Sperling, Susan Kelz. *Tenderfeet and Ladyfingers: A Visceral Approach To Words And Their Origins.* New York: Viking, 1981.

The American Heritage Dictionary of the English Language. William Morris, Editor. New York: American Heritage Publishing and Houghton Mifflin, 1969.

The Random House Dictionary of the English Language. Stuart Berg Flexner, Editor-In-Chief. New York: Random House, 1987.

Thomas, Lewis. *The Medusa and the Snail: More Notes of A Biology Watcher.* New York: Viking, 1979.

Tuchman, Barbara W. *The March of Folly: From Troy To Vietnam.* New York: Ballantine Books, 1984.

Vanoni, Marvin. *Great Expressions.* London: Grafton Books, 1989.

Webster's Word Histories. Frederick C. Mish, Editor. Springfield, MA: Merriam-Webster Inc., 1989.

Word Histories & Mysteries. Editors Of The American Heritage Dictionaries. Boston: Houghton Mifflin, 1986.

expiring, 172
export, 118
extending, 54
extorted, 112
extrovert, 115

facere, 75
fall, 2
false, 22
falsehood, 22
familia, 37
familiar, 37
family, 37
famulus, 37
faran, 169
fari, 3
farewell, 169
farm, 128
farmer, 128
fasces, 132
Fasci 'd Combattimento, 132
fascina, 132
fascinare, 133
fascinated, 133
fascine, 132
fascinum, 133
Fascinus, 133
fascis, 132
fascism, 132
faux pas, 33
felix qui nihil debet, 11
fell, 6
fence, 22
fer, 161
feroc, 49
ferocious, 49
ferre, 161, 165
fet, 34
fetter, 34
feu, 170
ficare, 85
figere, 158
fin, 168
finality, 168
finalized, 168
finare, 168

fine, 168
fineness, 170
finessed, 170
fingerhut, 147
finis, 168
firm, 128
firma, 128
firmare, 128
firms, 128
firth, 6
fish, 7
fjall, 6
fjord, 6
fjoturr, 34
flumen, 153
flumes, 153
foglio, 121
folium, 121
fondre, 156
font, 156
foot, 32
fot, 34
found, 156
foundation, 157
foundry, 156
fox, 148
fragor, 166
franc, 5
francus, 5
Franglais, 5
frank, 5
Frankfurt am Main, 142
frankfurter, 142
Franko, 5
Frankreich, 5
Franks, 5
frater, 9
fraternities, 9
Frederick I, 110
ful, 2, 68
Fuller, John, 116
fundamental, 157
fundare, 156
fundere, 156
funds, 157
furlang, 113
furlong, 113

furrow, 113
fusion, 156

Gabor, Zsa Zsa, 40
Gaels, 7
gage, 89
galapagos, 122
gamma, 102
Gardini, Caesar, 140
Garfield, James, 47
garnir, 126
garnishing, 126
Garten, 107
gauche, 25
gel, 155
gelo, 155
gen, 105
gendarme, 108
gener, 106
generare, 105
generate, 105
generic, 107
generous, 107
genes, 107
Genesis, 107
geneticists, 107
genitalia, 107
genius, 107
Genoa, 152
gens d'armes, 108
gentiles, 107
gentle, 107
gentlemen, 108
genu, 106
genuine, 106
genus, 106
geolo, 155
George IV, 104
gerbh, 102
gerrymander, 166
gharsati, 159
ghel, 155
gher, 159
gheu, 156
gholt, 155
ghrei, 159

salere, 16
salsa, 16
salt, 16
Salt River, 18
saltcellar, 17
salted, 142
Salzburg, 16
sandwich, 141
Sartre, Jean Paul, 13
Saturnalia, 171
Saturnian Hill, 134
Saturnus, 171
sauce, 16
saucer, 16
sausage, 16
sause, 16
saussiche, 142
sawbuck, 30
Saxons, 6
scarified inscriptions, 103
scarifying, 103
Schurke, 67
schurken, 67
Schwyz, Switzerland, 161
Scott, Walter, 104
Scotch, 139
scratching, 103
scribble, 105
scribe, 102
scribere, 102
script, 102
Scriptures, 103
scutarius, 98
seax, 6
Seaxan, 6
secuts, 37
sedan, 77
sedere, 77
seducing, 100
selection, 93
semi, 35
sen, 101
senators, 101
senatus, 101
senile, 101
senilis, 101
sergant, 100
serge de Nimes, 152

sergeants, 100
sergent, 100
serjant, 100
serjaunt, 100
serjeant, 100
servient, 100
servire, 100
servus, 100
sesqui, 35
sesquipedality, 35
shabata, 2, 29
Shakespeare, Willam, 53, 64,
  107, 109, 120, 147
shark, 66
Shaw, Bernard, 39, 122, 170
shell out, 88
sherry, 144
shire, 141
shirk, 67
shrimp, 67
Shylock, 120
sideburns, 80
sign, 98
signare, 98
silhouette, 63
Silhouette, Etienne de, 63
sincerely, 169
sinister, 24
sit(os), 44
sittan, 77
skribh, 102
slave, 100
sleuth, 20
sleuthhound, 20
slimy, 120
slithy, 120
sloth, 20
sluice, 153
Smith, Sydney, 139
smog, 120
sneigwh, 8
sophism, 106
sophisma, 106
sophisticated, 106
sophomore, 3, 106
sophos, 3, 106
Soviet, 136
specere, 124

specula, 124
specular, 124
speculative, 124
spend, 39
spendo, 39
spirare, 172
spokespersons, 41
spondere, 39
sponge, 67
sponsorship, 39
sports, 119
spouses, 39
spuse, 39
sta, 96, 99
stabilis, 97
stability, 97
stablire, 97
stacyonere, 95
stagnant, 97
stagnum, 97
stan, 96
stand, 96
stand by, 96
  for, 96
  on one's two feet, 96
  one-night, 96
  one's ground, 96
  out, 96
  pat, 96
standing, 97
stank, 97
stantia, 96
Stanton, Will, 163
stanza, 96
starboard, 118
stare, 85, 95
stari, 85
stasis, 96
state, 97
states, 97
stationarius, 95
stationary, 95
stationery, 95
statista, 97
statistics, 97
statisticum, 97
Statistik, 97
statuary, 96